Roots in
the Rhineland

America's German Heritage
in Three Hundred Years
Of Immigration
1683–1983

Christine M. Totten

German Information Center

A publication of the
German Information Center
410 Park Avenue
New York, N.Y. 10022

©1983 German Information Center
410 Park Avenue, New York, N.Y. 10022
ISBN: 0-912685-01-8

Produced by Fred Weidner & Son Printers, Inc.
Design by Creative Images in Inc., in N.Y.C.

Roots in The Rhineland

1. Beginnings in Germantown 5
The German-Americans 1683-1883-1983 6
The German Mayflower 7
Forerunners 8
The Founding of Germantown 9

2. Contributions to American Life 11
Craftsmen, Printers, and Inventors 12
German Newspapermen in America 14
Sacred Music in the Wilderness 16
German-American Harmonies 19
From Edification to Entertainment 24
The Cloister and the Bauhaus 26
Folk Art and Fine Arts 27
Men of Letters 31
America's Schoolteachers 34
Men of God in American Churches 41
Reluctant Involvement in Politics 48
Pacifists and Soldiers 52
Early Humanitarian Concern 56
Joys of the Good and Simple Life 60
Family Ties 63

3. Present-Day Heritage 65
New Life in Old Organizations 66
The 1950's: Era of Encounters 68
Different Traits in a Familiar Image 72
Germantown's Heirs 75

Acknowledgments 76
Index 77

BEGINNINGS
IN GERMANTOWN

1

The German-Americans
1683 • 1883 • 1983

The Germans are among the oldest and largest ethnic groups in America. Thirty-three settlers from Krefeld in the Rhineland who sailed to Philadelphia in 1683 were the forerunners of more than seven million immigrants from the German-speaking countries.

A century ago, in 1883, the German-American community in the United States was at its peak of growth. In the early 1880's its self-confidence as a group was boosted by up to a quarter of a million newcomers every year. On October 6, 1883, the arrival of the first substantial contingent of Germans on American soil two hundred years earlier was commemorated with countless Bicentennial celebrations all over the country.

The German-Americans were proud of their accomplishments. They saw themselves as counterparts to the Massachusetts Pilgrims and called the *Concord*, the ship that had carried the first of the pioneers, the "German Mayflower." They looked upon Francis Daniel Pastorius, the founder of the earliest settlement in Germantown, as the "Moses of his people."

The pattern of German immigration consisted of waves of arrivals that recurred at steady intervals for over three centuries. With the exception of religious sects like the Amish, the Germans were most willing to be assimilated into the American mainstream. In the course of the last hundred years they consequently lost many of the characteristics of a self-contained, coherent ethnic entity; at the same time, however, they continued to grow in numbers. Government-sponsored surveys of 1979 and 1980 reveal that 52 million Americans trace their descent to German-speaking countries. Germans outnumber not only the Irish with 43.7 million but also the 40 million English.

On October 6, 1983, the celebrations of the Tricentennial of German immigration are no longer an affair dedicated exclusively to German-Americans. They cause the American people as a whole to examine a part of their heritage that has formed a solid pillar of the country's growth for the last three centuries. The German element in America supplied down-to-earth hard work in a quiet, inconspicuous way. It also contributed specific ideas and values in building America.

The Germans in Germantown at the end of the 17th century showed traits that characterize German immigration up to the present day. They provided brains as well as brawn. Spiritual and intellectual leaders stimulated scholarly discourse. Masses of common folk patiently cultivated American soil. With their skill in the crafts and trades they enhanced their adopted country's wealth. German immigrants brought musical and artistic talent. They were in demand as teachers. They enriched the American way of life with their love for fairs and fun, and with their ability to celebrate as hard as they worked. And while they may have lacked political and economic assertiveness, they nonetheless spoke up as a group on matters of ethical and humanitarian concern.

The German Mayflower

Concord, the name of the English schooner on which the first German settlers sailed, was considered an appropriate symbol for the immigrants' friendly cooperation with the English and Dutch aboard. All of the passengers were attached to religious associations outside the established churches. They answered William Penn's call to share the "Holy Experiment" of his Quaker colony as settlers on the huge land grant which Penn's father had received for his services to the English crown.

As he greeted the newcomers at the port of Philadelphia, the "City of Brotherly Love," William Penn was accompanied by a young German lawyer, Francis Daniel Pastorius, who had become a close friend of the Proprietor of the colony since his arrival a month and a half earlier, on August 20, 1683. Pastorius was a scholarly and widely traveled man who spoke six languages—not including English. He had learned about William Penn's recruiting visits to the Rhineland in 1671 and 1677 from Dr. Spener's circle of Pietists, a group of religious, refined and affluent citizens of Frankfurt on the Main.

Known as the "Quiet in the Land," the Pietists had purchased 25,000 acres from William Penn and were enthusiastic about settling in the welcoming Quaker province. Pastorius tells us that "this begat a desire in my soul to continue in their society, and with them to lead a quiet, godly, and honest. life in a howling wilderness." Yet Pastorius' wish was to be fulfilled under quite different circumstances.

None of the upper-class Pietists of the "Frankfurt Land Company" ever followed their agent Pastorius to the promised land. Instead he became the leader of thirteen more modest families of settlers from Krefeld who had previously bought 18,000 acres of Penn's land. They came from that part of the Lower Rhine where German and Dutch traditions, dialects, and family names mingled in an inextricable way. The city of Krefeld, famous for the manufacture of linen and silk, prided itself as a haven of tolerance during the religious wars of the 17th century. Baptist sects, regarded with suspicion elsewhere, found refuge here. When changes in the overlordship of the region caused this spirit of friendly acceptance to deteriorate, the most enterprising among the Mennonite and Quaker families decided to accept William Penn's invitation. In his colony their freedom of conscience was guaranteed.

Pastorius visited the two groups of emigrants who were to join him in Pennsylvania on the way from Frankfurt to Rotterdam, his port of embarkation. In the hamlet of Kriegsheim in the left-bank Palatinate, he promised a few Quaker families to serve as their agent. He met the major group of his future companion settlers when he interrupted his travel down the Rhine and walked six miles on foot from the river to Krefeld on April 11.

Pastorius now was in charge of thirty-three Krefelders, the Kriegsheimers, and his own small party of servants who soon became property owners in their new country. These three groups were the original components of Germantown, the first sizable, stable, distinctly German settlement in America.

Forerunners

Long before 1683, Germans had taken an active part in the development of the new lands across the ocean. The ship on which Pastorius preceded the Krefelder settlers was called *America*, a coincidence that holds special meaning.

Almost 200 years before his crossing, a countryman of Pastorius, the cosmographer Martin Waldseemüller from Freiburg, had christened the new continent "America" in 1507, mistakenly crediting Amerigo Vespucci instead of Christopher Columbus with the discovery.

The fate of the first individual German settlers in the Jamestown colony in Virginia in 1607 is not known. It is recorded, however, that they provided the solid craftsmanship which Captain John Smith sorely missed among the English gentlemen of his group.

More colorful are the lives of two colonial leaders who stand out as distinct personalities among the German-Americans before Pastorius' time. Peter Minuit, originally Minnewit from Wesel in the Rhineland, is remembered for his purchase of the island of Manhattan from the Indians for sixty Dutch guilders, approximately twenty-four dollars in gold. His career as director of the thriving colony of New Netherland ended in 1629. But he returned six years later with 50 Swedish settlers and founded Fort Christina on the Delaware.

The second governor of the New Amsterdam colony, Jacob Leisler, also came from Frankfurt, Pastorius' point of departure. Unlike the mild-mannered Pietist, Leisler was a rebel. Historians agree that he was the first independent-minded politician in the colonies who demanded unity and severance of ties with London. Hanged by the British in Manhattan in 1691, he was posthumously vindicated by Parliament, and his fortune restored to his family.

The Founding of Germantown

In the turbulent first century of the American colonies, the settlers from Krefeld and Kriegsheim were fortunate to start out under the leadership of a trained negotiator like Pastorius.

When the terrain originally assigned to them was too mountainous for the pioneers from the flat lands of the Rhine plain, Pastorius won a parcel of land six miles north of Philadelphia that pleased them. Pastorius was the temporary host for over twenty of his newly arrived countrymen in his own tiny hut. It had oiled paper instead of window glass but boasted a whimsical Latin inscription. His motto: "Good friends are welcome in my wretched abode, but the profane better keep out" made even serious-minded William Penn laugh.

Caves were hollowed out in the ground, and covered as miserable shelters for the first winter. With wry humour, Pastorius reports that the new settlement's name "Germantown" was rhymed with "Armentown," town of the poor. "We called the place Germantown," he wrote, "which to us signifies likewise the City of Brothers; some gave it the name Armentown, because many of the aforesaid settlers could not procure themselves a provision for even a few weeks, much less months. And it cannot, it will never be described in sufficient detail nor adequately believed by our more prosperous descendants in what poverty this Germantown started out, but at the same time in which cheerful Christian serenity and indefatigable hard work it was all begun."

Germantown's nickname was soon made obsolete by the skills of its craftsmen. At their first sale in Philadelphia in 1684, the products of their spinnning, linen weaving and dyeing netted only a disappointing 10 thalers. But as Pastorius had foreseen, the blue-flowered flax soon proved the cure of Germantown's poverty. When Pastorius' letters to friends at home about life in Pennsylvania succeeded in bringing over more of his countrymen, Germantown became comfortably well-to-do.

They came from Krefeld and Mülheim on both sides of the lower Rhine, and from the Rhenish Palatinate upstream. Around Germantown these "High and Low Germans" who spoke High and Low German dialects were also frequently called the "High and Low Dutch." The Word "Dutch" sounded like "Deutsch," as the settlers called themselves. It was not always easy for the older immigrants from England to distinguish between newcomers from Germany and from Holland. In the 18th century, frequent reference to the newly arrived large groups of German farmers from the Palatinate as the "Pennsylvania Dutch" made the terms "German" and "Dutch" even more widely interchangeable in common American usage.

A decade after it was founded, the "German Township" consisted of 5,700 acres. It was divided into four parts: Germantown in the South, Crisheim, named for the home of the Palatine Quakers, Sommerhausen, in honor of Pastorius' birthplace in Franconia, and Crefeld, after the hometown of the core of the settlers.

By the end of the 17th century, Germantown had a wide and attractive Main Street, lined by peach trees. Over fifty families grew flowers and vegetables on three-acre lots of rich black ground. Fields north and south of town, orchards, vineyards, and beehives established the reputation of the Germans as expert farmers among their English and Scotch-Irish neighbors.

CONTRIBUTIONS TO AMERICAN LIFE

2

Craftsmen, Printers, and Inventors

Farming was a necessity for the first German settlers in Pennsylvania. It became a major occupation of the German-Americans in the next two centuries. By 1910 it was estimated that they had developed more than 672,000 farms in the United States with a total area of a hundred million acres. The citizens of Germantown, however, stressed that they were primarily craftsmen. Pastorius demonstrated that his people made their living from grapes, flax, and trade when he designed the official seal of his town in the shape of a three-leaf clover with a grapevine, a flax blossom, and a weaver's spool. One craft led to another. An early resident of Philadelphia wrote the following rhyme: "From linen rags good paper does derive, the first trade keeps the second trade alive...Convenience does appear to place them nigh, one in Germantown, t'other hard by. A paper mill near Germantown does stand . . ."

This important secondary industry, the first paper mill in America, was founded by William Rittenhouse. Born near Mülheim in the Rhineland, he was both Germantown's paper manufacturer and the community's first elected Mennonite preacher and bishop.

A prominent use of Rittenhouse's fine paper was made in Germantown at the press of Christopher Saur, an immigrant from North Germany. Saur used his technical gifts in many fields. He invented optical instruments, preceding other German lens-grinders like John J. Bausch from Württemberg and Henry Lomb from Hesse-Kassel, who set up their optical firm in Rochester, New York, in 1855. Perfecting cast-iron stoves, Saur opened up an industry in which his countryman Baron Stiegel excelled. He had bought Johann Huber's first iron foundry in Pennsylvania in 1788, and laid out Manheim in Lancaster county in the pattern of his home town. In the 19th century, Henry Clay Frick and Charles Schwab, Andrew Carnegie's first lieutenant in Pittsburgh, followed as experts in iron manufacture.

Saur, the all-around inventor, was to be best remembered as an innovative printer who carried on the tradition of Johannes Gutenberg, his 15th-century countryman from Mainz. Like Gutenberg, Saur experimented successfully with the manufacture of printing type and ink. His publication of the Lutheran Bible was a historic achievement. It came out in 1743 with 1,272 pages in its original German. At the time, the first English Bible in America had yet to be printed, since Oxford University still held the copyright.

Christopher Saur, printer, technical inventor, editor, and journalist, appears at the beginning of a long line of similarly talented Americans from Germany. In Saur's lifetime, one of them was Henry Miller who announced the ratification of the Declaration of Independence in his *Staatsbote* ahead of other papers and later became the printer for Congress.

Saur lost one of his print shop's best customers in the course of a personal feud with Conrad Beissel. The gifted and headstrong Beissel came to Pennsylvania from Eberbach near Heidelberg where he was born as the posthumous son of a baker and notorious drinker. After he became the leader of a Baptist sect and founded the Dunkers' cloister for men and women at Ephrata in 1732, Beissel was attacked in Saur's papers. Saur denounced Beissel as a servant of Mars for his severity, and of Venus because of his attraction for women. Beissel had won Saur's wife Maria as "Solitary Sister Marcella" for his "Economy". She returned to her family after fifteen years, but Beissel had by then set up his own print shop for ornate hymnals on the premises at Ephrata. J. Gottfried Seelig, one of the Brethren of the mystic Rosicrucian sect "from the Ridge" near Germantown, instructed Beissels' monks in the art of bookbinding.

The making of books and the perfection of the printed page continued to be a favorite domain of craftsmen and inventors from Germany in the following centuries. The engineer who took a major step in the modernization of Gutenberg's invention, Ottmar Mergenthaler, derived strong idealistic satisfaction from his accomplishment. Mergenthaler was the son of a village teacher in Württemberg. As an immigrant toolmaker in Baltimore he could not forget that "at home we had no money for school books." He was possessed by the idea of eliminating the costly setting of type by hand because he wanted "more books-more education for all." He secured his Linotype invention with 50 patents in 1886—"a line o'type" as his supporter Reid of the *New York Tribune* spontaneously called the product from Mergenthaler's machine that constantly set, melted, and recast its letters at the touch of a finger.

In Mergenthaler's generation, German-American names cropped up again among the lithographers who illustrated the printed work, and eventually among the forerunners of a technology that was to replace it electronically. Herman Hollerith's name is remembered with the punch card system that he invented at the end of the 19th century.

German Newspaper-men in America

Benjamin Franklin estimated in 1766 that one third of Pennsylvania's population was German, and he worried about the preponderance of Germans in the printing business and in the legislature. Franklin's *Philadelphische Zeitung*, America's first German-language paper, failed in 1732. "The German Inhabitants of the Province of Pennsylvania" whom Franklin addressed in a matter-of-fact tone were turned off by the Roman type of his paper.

Seven years later, when Christopher Saur appealed to the "well inclined readers" of his *Hoch Deutsch Pennsylvanischer Geschicht Schreiber* in the more familiar Gothic lettering and fancy initials, his paper had astounding success. At first a monthly journal which supported Quaker pacifist policies, it became a weekly in 1773 and reached a circulation of over 4,000.

In the same decade in which Saur started his newspaper, Peter Zenger, another German printer-turned-journalist, rendered an important service to American concepts of liberty in his *New York Weekly Journal*. Zenger belonged to a sector of German immigration that faced greater hardships than the emotionally and materially more secure sectarians of Germantown. The farmers who had left the Palatinate on both sides of the Rhine escaped famines caused by the scorched-earth policies of Louis XIV's generals. Around 1710, 2,814 of them crossed the Atlantic at the expense of Queen Anne's helpful government. In overcrowded, typhoid-plagued ships, Peter Zenger's father was one of 446 who died on the way. The thirteen year-old boy had to shoulder the responsibility for his family after his arrival in New York.

When he became printer and editor of the *Journal*, Zenger fearlessly attacked the corrupt practices of New York's Governor Cosby. Although he was arrested and put behind bars, Zenger continued to direct his newspaper with the courageous efforts of his wife, Anna. In a historic court case of 1735, Philadelphia's famous lawyer, Andrew Hamilton, pleaded successfully for truth as the decisive criterion in the libel suit against the editor. In acquitting Peter Zenger, the jury established the principle of freedom of the press.

Peter Zenger had fought his high-principled journalistic battles in English. The German-language press that began to flourish after him was mainly concerned with more modest issues of a local German community or church. The German-American statesman Carl Schurz defined as the four major purposes of a German paper that it should explain America, promote cooperation among its readers, inform them of developments in Germany, and impress the German immigrants with the "open-handed generosity" of the United States.

Like almost half of the émigrés from the German revolutionary movements after 1830 and 1848, Carl Schurz, the most prominent of the revolutionaries known as "Forty Eighters," proved himself as a journalist in his new country. His pen was in demand both for English and German-language periodicals like the *New York Tribune*, the *Detroit Post*, and St. Louis' *Westliche Post*. After his term as Secretary of the Interior, Schurz accepted Henry Villard's invitation to become editor of the *New York Evening Post*. Heinrich Hilgard from Speyer had started his new life as a reporter for the *New Yorker Staats-Zeitung* in 1858 with the name Henry Villard. Schurz noted that Villard remained an enthusiastic idealist after he had become one of the most influential railroad entrepreneurs in the United States.

Successful newspaper work was a common bond between Carl Schurz, the politician, Henry Villard, the tycoon of the Northern Pacific Railroad, Gustav Koerner, the diplomat and lawyer, and representatives of virtually all of the Forty-Eighters' professions. Journalism also became a professional platform for women, among them feminists like Mathilde T. Wendt and, especially, Mathilde Giesler Anneke. Carl Schurz stressed Mathilde Anneke's noble character, her beauty, vivacity, and ardent patriotism. She had followed her husband, the officer and journalist Fritz Anneke, on horseback into the military camp of the revolutionaries. Her emancipatory *Frauenzeitung* in Cologne was followed by the *Deutsche Frauenzeitung* in Milwaukee in 1852 after her arrival in the U.S.A. Karl Heinzen, a vigorous spokesman for social change, shared Mathilde Anneke's revolutionary ideals in favor of women's suffrage and spread them in his numerous German-language publications.

The effect of the émigrés' radical demands was limited by the small circulation of their papers. The fast-growing conventional German-language press of their time frowned upon feminists and social reformers.

By 1800, some 38 different German-language papers had appeared in Pennsylvania alone. With the increase of the German population in the cities of the "German Belt" in the Midwest, daily papers proliferated. Cincinnati's *Volksblatt* was founded in 1836. In Chicago, St. Louis, and Milwaukee, the German-language papers caught up with New York, where the *Staats-Zeitung* had tripled its subscriptions in five years, reaching 15,300 in 1856. In 1855, 79% of all foreign-language periodicals in the United States were German. The all-time peak was reached in 1894, when over 800 different German papers were published.

After a gradual decline, these figures plummeted toward the end of the First World War. In the 1920's only 278 were left, many of them mouthpieces of small organizations. In the late 1930's one of these newsletter-type papers grew into an important publication with worldwide circulation under the direction of a master journalist. Manfred George transmitted the journalistic brilliance of Berlin's "Golden Twenties" to New York. As editor of the German-Jewish weekly *Aufbau*, George created a forum for the refugees from Hitler. After 1945, his periodical served as a focus of interest in the postwar democratic development of the Federal Republic. At the same time, George interpreted American politics and culture for German readers in West German publications. His familiarity with the contemporary American and German scene made him a pivot of cultural communication across the Atlantic, and the effect of his work was intensified by the continuity provided by his successor, Dr. Hans Steinitz.

Sacred Music in the Wilderness

Friends of music were good customers of Germantown's first printers. The love of song was characteristic of the close-knit religious groups which were a chief component of German immigration, up to 19th century utopian societies like the Rappite Harmonists.

The Baptist sects appeared as true heirs of the musical heritage of the German Reformation. Martin Luther encouraged his congregations to sing joyfully in the Hebrew tradition of the sacred song. In contrast, the Puritans in New England banned music from their austere services and declared that singing was for the chosen in heaven alone. Pennsylvania's Quakers also preferred to do without music in their meetings. When German religious leaders in the colonies followed Luther's example, they opened up a new chapter in the unfolding of American culture.

The first elaborate use of music at a special ecclesiastical event is reported from November 24, 1703, when Justus Falkner, a young deacon from Saxony, was ordained a Lutheran minister of the Swedish Gloria Dei church on the Delaware. The Theosophist Brethren near Germantown were good friends of Falkner, who wrote some of their favorite revivalists hymns. They played the "viol, hautboy, trumpets, and kettle drums" at his ordination. The leader of their Rosicrucian sect, Magister John Kelpius, even brought a small organ, which most likely had accompanied his immigration in 1694.

The members of Kelpius' esoteric sect, "The Society of the Woman in the Wilderness," earned the suspicion of their neighbors with the use of divining rods and horoscopes. They explained that they came to Germantown because here one could be "peasant, scholar, priest, and nobleman all at the same time and without interference." Some of them held degrees in theology. Kelpius received his doctorate in Philosophy at the age of 16. The unhealthy dampness of his hermit's cave on the Wissahickon River ended his pursuit of composing sacred music when he died at 31.

The main heir of Kelpius' pioneering work in music was not, however, a scholar but rather a self-made musical enthusiast. Conrad Beissel, the musician, was evoked by Thomas Mann when he wrote *Dr. Faustus* in American exile. In his youth, Beissel played the fiddle for dances in the Neckar Valley, but his extraordinary organizational and musical talents appeared only after he became the head of the Dunkers' sect at Ephrata Cloister. Brother Peter Müller, the eventual successor of "Vater Friedsam" or "Peaceloving Father," as he was called, wrote to Benjamin Franklin about Beissel: "The master of that Angelic Art will be astonished to see that therein a man, destitute of all human Instruction, came therein to the highest pitch of Perfection, merely through his own Industry . . ."

Beissel's lack of theoretical schooling did not prevent him from writing a treatise on harmony. His hymns, over four hundred in one hymnal alone, were his own creations in word, tune, and choral arrangement. They were written in as many as seven vocal parts, and edited under lush Baroque titles like "Play of Paradisical Delight" or "The Cooing of Solitary Turtledoves in the Wilderness." Beissel's major anthology with a thousand hymns, the *Zionist Incense Hill*, still exists in 56 copies in contemporary libraries.

As a musical director Beissel succeeded in his wish to make his choirs the "firstlings of America." With an almost Wagnerian sense for theatrical effects, Beissel had his singing school meet at night. Robed in pure white, the five small choirs of Brothers and Sisters were echoed by voices up on the gallery that floated "like voices of angels" through the candlelit assembly hall, the *Saal*. "The whole neighborhood," Peter Müller tells, "was touched by the sound of this heavenly music."

More effective in their impact on the musical advancement of the colonies than the inward-directed German mystics, like the Dunkers and Schwenkfelders, were their missionary, outgoing countrymen from Herrnhut, Saxony. Their leader, Count Zinzendorf, was a man of the world. On his estate in in Herrnhut, he had given refuge to the "hidden seed," the last members of the ancient protestant church "Unitas Fratrum," long persecuted in Bohemia and Moravia. He became a convert, reorganized and enlarged the group, and motivated it with a missionary zeal that is alive in the "Moravian Church" on three continents to this day. Zinzendorf shared the gifts of Beissel and Kelpius as a composer of hymns. In his efforts to evangelize the Indians in Georgia and Pennsylvania, he used the influence of music on the human soul. Herrnhut's hymnody affected not only the Indians. John Wesley, the founder of Methodism, and his brother Charles learned to appreciate the faith of the Moravian Brethren and the power of their chorales on a stormy voyage to Savannah, Georgia, in 1736. Consequently, many of the themes and melodies found in the *Herrnhuter Gesangbuch* appeared in the early Methodist hymns.

The Moravians were eminently practical. Men of means, they set up flourishing industries for their customary Old World needs, from buttons to bells. They established public water works in Bethlehem, their settlement in Pennsylvania since 1741. They imported a fire engine from England,

and provided a pharmacy when Dr. Frederick Otto opened his *Apotheke* in 1743.

The Brethren were equally efficient in running their "Collegium Musicum," America's first regular music school. In 1744, the Herrnhuter brought over professionally trained music teachers from Saxony. They ordered special violas and flutes from Germany for the proper celebration of Christmas. When George Washington visited the Brethren and commended them for their efforts "to civilize and Christianize the savages of the wilderness", he was greeted by "several melodies . . . played on trumpets, French horns, and trombones."

Among major compositions imported to America by the Moravians, the *Mass in B-Minor* by Johann Sebastian Bach stands out. To this day, the traditional affinity of the Moravians for Bach attracts friends of Baroque music to their festivals, especially the Easter sunrise services in Winston-Salem and Bethlehem.

The building of an organ on American soil goes back to 1737, the year after the arrival of the Moravians. The skills of its builder, Brother Johann Gottfried Klemm, soon were so much in demand that he had to send overseas for an assistant. Musicians' and cabinetmakers' talents, both regarded as typically German, were needed also for the manufacture of pianofortes. It became a domain of German immigrants in the 19th century. Names like Knabe, Weber and even Wurlitzer, are hardly remembered any more. But the company founded by Heinrich Engelhard Steinweg, who came to New York from Brunswick in 1850 with four sons, continues to produce the Steinway grands which remain the pride of the American concert hall.

German-American Harmonies

Immigrants from many lands contributed to the melting pot of American musical creativity. A specifically American form of musical culture emerged in the 19th century, at a time when the German element in the United States was most active and effective in shaping musical tastes and traditions. The memory of conductors and musicians from Germany, who smoothed the transition from the simple intrumental accompaniment of a frontier dance to the polish and perfection of the modern concert hall, is still anchored in American historical consciousness. The special relationship between American and German music has been renewed by a process of musical give-and-take between the United States and Germany that continues.

The German influence on American musical development during its formative decades rested mainly on three pillars. First, the broad range of German musical activity made it all-pervasive. From the popular appeal of the bluecapped "little German band" on the street corner to the most ambitious symphonic orchestra, both lowbrow and highbrow tastes were satisfied. Second, German music was personified in a few great names that were highly visible on engagements all over the country, and which established personal links to contemporary German composers. Third, the deliberate attempt of the successful German conductors to decentralize American musical excellence found a response in the rise of midwestern cities to musical prominence. Local choirs and musical associations had prepared their way, especially in the "German Quadrangle" on the map of the United States, roughly within the lines connecting New York City, Minneapolis, St. Louis and Baltimore.

Up to the first third of the 19th century, musical societies in Philadelphia, New York, and Boston were unchallenged in their superior quality. Gottlieb Graupner, an oboe player from Hanover, who has been called "the father of American orchestral music," was among the leading figures of Boston's *Handel and Haydn Society*. Its members were sufficiently self-assured to ask Beethoven to compose an oratorio for their choir in 1823.

New York was the starting point for the Germania Orchestra with a core of 23 émigrés from the German revolution of 1848. It gave 829 concerts in its six years of existence and introduced Beethoven's *Ninth Symphony* as one of the all-time favorites of the American concert hall. The Germania Orchestra had its most fertile period after it disbanded in 1854. Wherever its former members settled, they formed a nucleus of musical activity in the tradition of German municipal orchestras.

The extension of America's musical awakening beyond the East Coast was initiated by Theodore Thomas, a native of Hanover. Thomas deliberately aimed to extend the advantages of cultural decentralization, as he knew them in his homeland, to his new country. After establishing his reputation as a conductor in New York City, Thomas reached out to the Middle West. He was appointed Head of the new Cincinnati College of Music in 1879. Invited to Chicago in 1891, he founded the orchestra which became the Chicago Symphony, and set up an opera company.

The effect of Thomas' work in the Midwest and South was intensified by Leopold Damrosch. The descendant of a Jewish family from Posen on the eastern outskirts of Prussia, Damrosch had represented musical excellence in the hinterland when he conducted an Oratorio Society and the Philharmonic Orchestra in Breslau. He was a personal friend of Clara Schumann, Franz Liszt, and Richard Wagner, and became an apostle of contemporary German music after his emigration to America. He put the newly founded Metropolitan Opera in New York on its feet financially with a German opera season in 1884. Damrosch's creation, the New York Symphony, aroused musical interest on long spring tours to the Middle West, the South, and eventually the Far West.

From Cleveland to Pittsburgh, from Chicago to Cincinnati, from Milwaukee to St. Louis, further west in Minneapolis and Kansas, far west in San Francisco, and south in far-off Texas, music lovers among geographic concentrations of German immigrants welcomed Thomas' and Damrosch's kindling of symphonic ambitions. The conductors' most enthusiastic allies were the German singing societies in the "German Belt" and in cities like Buffalo, Baltimore, Charleston, Columbus and Louisville. In our time of stereo cassettes, the *Männerchöre* have shrunk to a shadow of their former flamboyant existence. But a good many of them have passed their hundredth birthday and still give testimony to the German-Americans' perennial love for music, sociability, and conviviality.

In the 19th century the *Sängerbünde*, the singers' clubs, also demonstrated the Germans' unfortunate tendency to dissipate their social energies in ever smaller groups. Special German-American events made their inability to integrate in sizable organizations clearly visible: In Cincinnati eighteen major German clubs and six different choral societies contributed to the festivities at the unveiling of a monument to Frederick Hecker, the 1848er politician, in 1881.

In the 1880's, Cincinnati was at the peak of a choral development that dated back to 1846 when the city hosted its first *Sängerfest*, the regional competitive meeting of singing clubs. Cincinnati shared the title "Athens of the West," earned by its citizens' active involvement in amateur music and stage productions, with Milwaukee, the other center of German-American industry and culture. Kettledrums made out of brewers' kettles were the hallmark of Milwaukee's *Musikverein*, and the Pabst brewing family provided a permanent building for German-American concerts and theatre. Such lively cultural activities invited comparisons with Munich as the city of beer and the arts.

On the East Coast, German choral associations provided mass entertainment for tens of thousands with a repertoire that ranged from Bach and Mendelssohn to Stephen Foster and the *Star-Spangled Banner*. In 1876, the New York *Liederkranz* presented the Grand Centennial Inaugural March which Richard Wagner had composed for the event. The singers of the *Deutscher Liederkranz* looked back on a stormy history since their society was founded in 1847. Like many of its sister organizations, the choir suffered from quarrels among highly opinionated members that led to splits regarded as typically German by outsiders. When new works by Richard Strauss demanded a larger scope of the choir, a recommendation was made to add female voices. Dissenting members promptly separated from the *Liederkranz*, and formed an exclusive *Männerchor*. Under the directorship of Dr. Leopold Damrosch, this new *Arion* club became one of the famous choirs in America.

Walter Damrosch was the better known of two musician sons of Leopold. As a conductor and composer, the younger Damrosch completed his father's work as a proponent of German music in the difficult political climate of the 20th century. Theodore Roosevelt vouched for Walter Damrosch's "fervid Americanism" when the conductor was attacked as a Germanophile in World War I. In the 1920's, Damrosch began to use the radio for his musical mission. On many tours of Europe's capitals with his New York Symphony he proved that American orchestras could now compete with the best that Europe offered in symphonic music.

Guest concerts by American symphony orchestras have become an integral part of Germany's musical scene ever since. To this day, friends of music in the Federal Republic cherish the performances of the New York orchestra and of companies from Boston, Philadelphia, Cleveland, and

Chicago, the same municipal centers of excellence that received their first impulse from German immigrants over a century ago. As in the time of the Weimar Republic, the decentralization of cultural life in modern West Germany continues to serve many young American singers and instrumentalists as a springboard for their career in the United States. When Richard Wagner's grandson Wolfgang stepped on the stage of Bayreuth's festival house for rehearsals of the *Rheingold* in 1961, he suddenly recognized the prevalent nationality of his cast and exclaimed: "Is it possible that *all* of you are Americans?!" A year earlier, *Time* magazine ascribed the popularity of fifty professional combo groups and almost a thousand amateur jazz bands in West Germany to the influence of American military bands. Actually, German enthusiasm for ragtime and jazz had originated in the 1920's and all of Hitler's efforts to eradicate it only increased its appeal while it went underground.

A profound strengthening of American interest in German music was the effect of Hitler's persecution of Germany's most creative musical element. A large number of Austrians among the prominent émigré musicians increased the American tendency to disregard national borders in their view and appreciation of artistic contributions from the German-speaking countries. Whether they originated in Austria, Switzerland, or Germany, musical societies and individuals were lumped together as a part of German culture in American eyes.

In the 1930's, Berlin and Vienna stood out as the two centers of German music which composers, conductors and performers left as they fled Nazi oppression.

The careers of Paul Hindemith, Bruno Walter and Otto Klemperer were closely linked to Berlin. The composer and professor Hindemith moved from Berlin's Academy of Music to Yale University in 1940. The man of whom Albert Einstein said that he wrote music the way a tree bears fruit, had been expelled by the Nazis for his "degenerate art." Born in Berlin as Bruno Walter Schlesinger, Bruno Walter was at the height of a brilliant career both in Germany and the United States when he settled in California before World War II. The great interpreter of Mozart and Mahler, of Beethoven and Brahms, eventually conducted every major symphony orchestra in the United States. Otto Klemperer had to leave Berlin's Kroll Opera before he directed symphonies in New York and Los Angeles.

Erich Leinsdorf, Kurt Herbert Adler, and Arnold Schönberg came from Vienna. Erich Leinsdorf, Viennese by birth and training, served as conductor in the Metropolitan Opera, in Cleveland and in Boston. Kurt Herbert Adler had built his reputation in Germany before he emigrated to conduct opera in Chicago, San Francisco, and New York. Arnold Schönberg established the fame of his twelve-tone system while he shared his professional life between Vienna and Berlin. When he died in Los Angeles in 1951, fifteen of his significant works had been composed during the seventeen years of his American exile.

Among musical performers, the soprano Lotte Lehmann enjoyed high popularity as an opera singer and interpreter of German *Lieder*. She studied in her native Berlin, made Vienna her artistic home, found refuge in New York in 1938, and ended her career as leading vocal teacher at the Music Academy of the West in Santa Barbara.

Most of the refugee musicians were heirs or innovators of the classical tradition. The *Three Penny Opera*, written by Bertolt Brecht and Kurt Weill, experimented with new patterns. As an early counterpart to the American musical, it was a smash hit. It ran for almost a decade off-Broadway in the 1950's and 1960's.

From Edification to Entertainment

The singing societies of the 19th century succeeded in combining the edification of their listeners in recitals of serious music with entertainment by lighter fare. Their counterparts on the stage, the amateur theatrical societies of the German-American *Liebhabertheater*, did not achieve the same purpose. Their popular comedy and operetta evenings provided pleasure for participants and audiences in the Midwest, from Iowa to Texas. Yet their efforts to transplant the heritage of the classical German drama to America failed in the long run. Friedrich Schiller, the bard of freedom, was widely admired in mid-century America, and his hundredth anniversary in 1859 was celebrated all over the country. But the directors of the German-language stage never competed with the great English dramatic tradition; they rather promoted Shakespeare's plays.

With the progress of dramatic production from the stage to the screen, a new field of artistic cooperation between the United States and Germany emerged. One of America's first film empires was established by Carl Laemmle, founder of the *Universal Pictures* company. He came from Swabia to Chicago in 1904 and opened there his first movie theatre. Among the films of his later production in Hollywood, the antiwar drama based on Erich Maria Remarque's novel *All Quiet on the Western Front* became a classic in 1930.

By this time, German names were firmly established in Hollywood. Again, many actors and producers came from Berlin and from Vienna and again, a major influx of exceptional talent was triggered by Nazi purges of the arts and by racial persecution in the 1930's.

Actor and film-director Ernst Lubitsch was born in Berlin and learned his trade there under Max Reinhardt. He worked in the United States after 1921, and excelled in elegant comedy. Another Berliner, Marlene Dietrich, also made her mark in smooth elegance and cosmopolitan sophistication. Worlds apart from the stereotype of the homebound and homely German "hausfrau," she was nonetheless teased as a "Kraut" by her good friend Ernest Hemingway. The star who used her Berlin accent to best advantage as Lola-Lola in Josef von Sternberg's *Blue Angel* could afford to shock her American fans by tracing her professional perfectionism to a Prussian upbringing in Berlin.

Film directors Otto Preminger and Billy Wilder represented Vienna in Hollywood. The Viennese Fritz Lang was among those innovators of the screen who had achieved distinction in Berlin's film industry before they emigrated.

Most recent developments in the international film industry show that cinema, like music, continues to be a fertile field of American-German interaction. Television has brought contemporary American realities and fantasies into West German living-rooms, from *Sesame Street* to *Star Wars*. The "new wave" of German film makers has found recognition with an "Oscar" for Volker Schlöndorff's cinematic version of Günter Grass' novel *The Tin Drum* in 1980. Fassbinder, Herzog, and Syberberg are recognized by American foreign film buffs as powerful stimuli in the transatlantic dialogue on the alienation of modern man.

The Cloister
and the Bauhaus

In the lifetime of Pastorius and his Germantown pioneers, necessity dictated the priorities of building. The settlers in the nearby Pennsylvania Dutch farm country put all their resources into magnificent, solid barns. On the other hand, the relatively small and insignificant farm houses of the Pennsylvania Dutch were scorned since colonial times as the miserable abodes of misers.

The sectarians also made only modest investments in their houses of God. Instead of churches, they erected meeting houses in a spirit of unpretentiousness and practicality, shunning the display of architectural opulence by the established churches in Europe which they had left as dissenters.

Yet there was an example of grandeur in humility not far from Germantown. At a first glance, the *Saal*, the meeting house, and the dormitories which Conrad Beissel had erected for the Brothers and Sisters of the Dunkers' cloister in Ephrata seem to fit inconspicuously, scattered haphazardly, into the rolling hills of Lancaster County. Only a closer look reveals the stark beauty of understatement in purely functional, austere walls, raised to an astonishing height of four stories. The massive roofs and the unconventional arrangement of the windows, distributed sparingly and with pointed disregard for their outside symmetry and appearance, convey an abstract charm that has only recently been fully appraised. Ephrata's architectural message is akin to medieval models before its time, still visible in Cistercian churches without spires in Conrad Beissel's native Württemberg. Beissel's principles of construction were guided by a religious idea. When his meeting house was built from solid oak logs, Beissel faithfully followed the example of King Solomon's temple, as he found it described in the book of Kings. It fitted his own sectarian ideas that wooden pegs were used exclusively instead of iron nails so that there was no "tool of iron heard in the house while it was building".

The architecture of Ephrata Cloister, devoid of all idle decoration, remained an isolated phenomenon of colonial history. But accents on functionalism, simplicity, and solid craftsmanship reappeared centuries later as German imports when American universities granted refuge to the "Bauhaus" in the 1930's.

The masters and apprentices of the Bauhaus movement after the First World War had rediscovered the medieval approach to the arts through expertise in handicraft skills. As the close-knit community of their school moved from Weimar to Dessau and on to Berlin, it was held together by strong artistic beliefs in the laws of necessity within their object. When their progressive ideas aroused suspicion which escalated to oppression under the Nazi government, many members of the Bauhaus followed the master builders Walter Gropius and Ludwig Mies van der Rohe into exile in the United States. The revolution which the Bauhaus had initiated in Germany lasted fourteen years. It came to full fruition during decades of profound influence on American design and architecture, confirming Benjamin Franklin's observation that "America cultivates best what Germany brought forth." Sullivan's and Frank Lloyd Wright's ideas of strict functionalism were developed to perfection in the sleek beauty of the Bauhaus' plans for universities, skyscrapers, apartment houses and embassies.

The Bauhaus architecture took root both on the East Coast and in the Midwest. The Berlin-born Walter Gropius trained a generation of American architects at the Harvard School of Architecture between 1937 and 1952. Mies van der Rohe was the son of a stonemason in Aachen in the Rhineland. His appointment to the Armour Institute—now the Illinois Institute of Technology—in 1937 made Chicago the trendsetter for American big-city architecture. "The King", as he was known, the "poet of steel and glass", set monuments of his credo "less is more" from the campus of the Illinois Institute to the shimmering bronze elegance of the Seagram Building in New York. When President Kennedy chose Mies for his first award of the Medal of Freedom, he expressed a nation's appreciation. It was condensed into one sentence by *Newsweek* in 1969: "We have all studied at the Bauhaus."

Folk Art and Fine Arts

The Bauhaus message for America touched all facets of the arts. It was represented by a wide range of artists' personalities, from Josef Albers' painting and graphic design to his wife Anni's art weaving, from the poetic cubism of Lyonel Feininger's woodcuts to Marcel Breuer's tubular chair design.

Long before the emigration of the Bauhaus school, artistic gifts from Germany had reached America on two levels: through the self-expression of the unknown immigrant in folk art and amateur painting, and in works of professional German-American and American artists who had received training in the art academies of Düsseldorf and Munich.

In the solitude of their monastic cells, the Brothers and Sisters of Ephrata Cloister renewed the old art of illustration of sacred texts. They made their calligraphy, the Gothic fraktur lettering, the basis of a typical art form of the earliest German immigration. The colorful and intricate design in the illumination of Conrad Beissel's hymnals set an example for the surrounding countryside. From the Cloister's school the art of fraktur spread and flourished widely, mainly in Pennsylvania, Maryland, and Virginia, until the middle of the 19th century. Extended to figurative motifs, the calligraphy was enriched by stars, birds, and animals like the unicorn, the old symbol for purity and wisdom. It spilled over from family documents to the adornment of chests and cabinets, stoveplates and weathervanes, pottery and glass vessels, and the most prosaic tools.

The so-called "hex-signs," picturesque six-petaled flowers or geometric designs copied from Pennsylvania Dutch barns, are typical decorations for commercially reproduced souvenirs from sightseeing trips in Lancaster county. With their alleged power to ward off evil, they are considered part of the notorious superstitions of the Pennsylvania Dutch. The medallion-like patterns on Pennsylvanian barns have been explained historically as pre-Christian fertility symbols, identical to paintings still found on Bavarian and Swiss farm-buildings, simply satisfying joy in decoration.

Pennsylvania Dutch folk art, like Pennsylvania Dutch literature, has remained in a status of "colonial petrification" ever since it was imported from Germany. It preserved its original charm but refused to be changed and further developed by its new American surroundings. Originals and imitations of the always cheerful and often amusing Pennsylvania Dutch art are much in demand at present. The exhibition mounted for the Tricentennial year by the Philadelphia Museum of Art under the title: "The Pennsylvania Germans: A Celebration of their Art," was assured of wide popular appeal at a time of general American predilection for folk art.

At the end of the colonial period paintings by professional artists gained in importance. A German painter who found recognition as a full-time artist after he emigrated from Württemberg to Philadelphia was Johann Ludwig Krimmel. When he joined his brother's accounting firm in Philadelphia in 1810, his genre pictures won immediate acclaim because they radiated so convincingly Krimmel's delight in the vitality and the free spirit of his new country. His *Election Day of 1815* and *Fourth of July 1819*, his scenes of inns and dances, are brimming over with happy crowds, with relaxed and cheerful folk. In the same year when Krimmel was elected president of the Association of American Artists, he drowned in a millpond near Germantown, only 36 years old.

The generation of artists after Krimmel thrived on interaction with European traditions. After seeking inspiration in London, Rome, and Florence, America's aspiring young painters settled for Düsseldorf and Munich between 1830 and 1890. The art academy in Düsseldorf in the Rhineland opened the door to fame and fortune for Emmanuel Gottlieb Leutze and Albert Bierstadt. They had strikingly similar backgrounds and careers. Leutze came to Philadelphia from his native Württemberg as a nine-year-old. In 1841, at 24, he went back to Germany to develop his burgeoning talent at Düsseldorf, where German Romanticism had focused in Europe's most challenging art school. While Leutze grew in stature as a painter, he got deeply involved in German politics. His heart went all-out to the liberal revolutionary fighters of 1848. When the revolution failed, Leutze felt himself ever more deeply confirmed in American Republican pride. Expressing his patriotism in spirited oils, he created America's most frequently reproduced historical painting with *Washington Crossing the Delaware*. The Rhine was reflected in the landscape of his river, and in the faces of the General and his boatsmen he portrayed members of the American artists' colony in Düsseldorf. A copy, painted by Leutze in 1851, is still a major attraction of New York's Metropolitan Museum of Art. Eight years later, Leutze was called back to America. He was commissioned to decorate the southwest staircase of the Capitol Building in Washington with a large mural: *Westward the Course of Empire Takes Its Way.*

The honor of being asked to embellish the Capitol was shared by Albert Bierstadt when Congress bought two of his monumental paintings. Bierstadt had been one of Leutze's most successful students at the Düsseldorf art academy. He became the prophet of America's natural beauty as Leutze had made himself the exponent of America's heroic historical spirit. He also had arrived from Germany as a child, and returned to the Rhineland, close to his native Solingen, to study art. But unlike Leutze, Bierstadt did not stay in Düsseldorf. After four years of study, he moved back to the United States and American themes. He became one of the most highly admired and paid painters of the 1860's. His training in the traditions of German Romanticism had boosted Bierstadt's greatest asset: his appreciative eye for the luminous beauty of a pristine landscape and his perceptiveness for the majesty of the American wilderness. Bierstadt found his favorite objects on the American frontier, especially in the Rocky Mountains. Immediately after his return from Germany, he joined the expedition of Colonel Landers and brought back a rich harvest of drawings and paintings from surveying an overland wagon route to the Far West.

Bierstadt became the best known among two generations of painters who built the myth of the Old West. Most of them were linked to Germany either by family ties or by their studies in Düsseldorf, later in Munich.

The love affair of the Germans on both sides of the Atlantic with the Old West and the picturesque traditions of the Indians had been kindled by literature as well as art. German readers were fascinated by *Leatherstocking*, the hero of James Fenimore Cooper's novels, and the noble Red Men who moved in the beautiful landscapes of the Austrian Karl Postl, known under the name Charles Sealsfield. The last and most captivating of these authors was Karl May. His central figures Winnetou and Old Shatterhand made the prairie the dreamland of German teenagers. Karl May's perennial best-sellers and the Western film have ingrained the image of the land where the buffalo roam deep in German consciousness. In the contemporary Old West Clubs of the Federal Republic and their charter flights to the Rockies and beyond, this nostalgia, now over a century old, lives on.

In America, the fame of Bierstadt and of his homage to the West faded as fast as it came. His grandiose scenery was dubbed theatrical, as American taste turned from Düsseldorf to Paris and the French Impressionists toward the end of the 19th century. The appeal of the Munich art academy had a brief peak after the decline of the Düsseldorf school, but persisted with individual American artists. Immediately upon his return from Munich, Grant Wood painted *American Gothic* in his Midwest home, transposing Wilhelm Leibl's "Old Master" technique into an American classic.

As in music, 20th century relations between American and German art were a process of continuous give-and-take. The bold colors and visions of the German Expressionists, the works by Josef Albers, Max Beckmann, and Lyonel Feininger, carried to America's doorstep by émigrés half a century ago, continue to engage art critics and art lovers in fertile debate. It was sparked by representative showings of Expressionist art in the 1950's, and has proved its lasting ability to provoke strong opinions in very recent exhibitions.

On the other side of the Atlantic, the impact of American art on the German art scene is all-pervasive. With their latest trends, whether in pop-art, op-art, conceptual art or minimal art, all major modern American artists have been introduced to Europe at the *documenta* in Kassel, and they are widely represented in the ubiquitous municipal museums of modern art in the Federal Republic.

Men of Letters

The first German poet and writer of renown in the American colonies was the leader of the Germantown pioneers himself, Francis Daniel Pastorius. Much of his work is still waiting for up-to-date interpretation, even though a more recent anthology calls him one of the most important poets of early America. One of Pastorius' beautifully penned manuscripts that are crumbling away on browned paper in the archives of the Historical Society in Philadelphia has recently found a modern critical edition: *Deliciae Hortenses or Garden Recreations* of 1711 comments on the pleasures of gardening and beekeeping in prose and rhyme.

As soon as Pastorius was well settled in Germantown about 1690, he cultivated his poetic talents as diligently as he cultivated his garden. He accumulated a work of close to 500 poems and epigrams, proverbs, hymns, and typical Baroque rhymed dedications. In spite of his polyglot and cosmopolitan background, he lapsed at times into provincial mediocrity. As a rule, he wrote in German or English, but he composed with ease also in Latin, Dutch, French, and Italian.

To the end of his days he remained the alert European intellectual. He enlarged the small library that had accompanied his immigration by books from Frankfurt and Philadelphia. He was also his own librarian and listed his close to three hundred volumes, neatly dividing them into groups by size. He kept up-to-date in Continental and English religious thought, in philosophy, pedagogy, geography, mathematics, law, natural science, as well as in practical instruction for house, garden and sickbed.

Among Pastorius' forty-three prose works, his *Geographic Description of the Very Recently Founded Province of Pennsylvania* of 1700 stands out as a little-known classic of historical interest. It was compiled from letters and reports and describes "the poverty as well as the riches of the province." The young European, who had resented the inequities of the old feudal social structure and the vanity of the old world's pleasures, traces his steps in search of spiritual rejuvenation as part of William Penn's "Holy Experiment."

This theme also appears in parts of Pastorius' major work, the *Beehive*. Beginning in 1696, Pastorius collected casually, in volume after volume, whatever seemed worthwhile to him in knowledge, insight, and his own moral or humorous advice. It was destined mainly for the instruction and edification of his two sons. Switching among four languages, Pastorius created an equivalent of teaching by way of Great Books.

Pastorius' rather haphazard experiment with an encyclopedia of scholarship found a modern successor more than a century after the *Beehive*. The *Encyclopedia Americana*, an American adaptation of the German work of reference, the *Brockhaus*, was set up in 14 volumes by a political writer, Francis Lieber. He found exile in the United States in 1827 after he had supported the cause of liberty in battles against Napoleon, the Turkish oppressors of Greece, and German political reaction. Lieber's flight to America brought out his large potential as a thinker and writer. At Harvard, as a professor of political science at New York's Columbia University, and as President Lincoln's codifier of martial law in the Civil War, Lieber established scholarly fame. King Frederick William IV of Prussia tried in vain to win him back as a professor to the University of Berlin from where he had been expelled as a revolutionary student.

Among Lieber's fellow revolutionaries who found refuge in America around 1830, a group of intellectuals combined scholarly pursuits with the practical demands of their new country in Pastorius' fashion. These "Latin Farmers" of Illinois, Missouri, and Texas add a colorful segment to the mosaic of German immigration.

The "Latin Farmers" accepted the necessity of working with their hands as a matter of ideological pride in a land far away from European decadence. Life in America had also taught Pastorius to deplore the preponderance of Aristotelian logic in his university studies. He complained that it "never earned a loaf of bread," and he saw to it that his sons were apprenticed to a weaver and a shoemaker.

In his *Journey through Texas* of 1851, Frederick Law Olmsted gave an account of his surprise at finding educated and cultivated German families doing hard work in the farming district near New Braunfels: "You are welcomed by a figure in blue flannel shirt and pendant beard, quoting Tacitus, having in one hand a long pipe, in the other a butcher's knife... barrels for seats, to hear a Beethoven's symphony on the grand piano... a bookcase half filled with classics, half with sweet potatoes."

The experience of the "Latin Farmers" was repeated in the 20th century. When Hitler's persecutions reached liberal and socialist men of letters, they were especially vulnerable because their skills were tied to their mother-tongue and not easily marketable in exile. The playwright Carl Zuckmayer escaped from the hopelessness of the German refugee authors' colony in Hollywood and recaptured his emotional equilibrium raising chickens on a farm in Vermont. "Nowhere I got so closely acquainted with the fogs of depression as in this land of eternal spring," Zuckmayer wrote later about California.

Other writers found comfort in the West Coast's benign climate in their difficult financial and emotional circumstances. While even well-known German authors had a hard time making ends meet, some German film directors and stars in Hollywood were extremely well-off. The film version of Heinrich Mann's novel *Professor Unrat*, the *Blue Angel*, had started Marlene Dietrich on the road to fame. Yet in 1940 Heinrich Mann lived as just another poor German writer in Hollywood, three years after a Congressional survey showed Marlene Dietrich as the recipient of the fifth highest income in the United States.

Heinrich Mann and many fellow émigré men of letters like Stefan Zweig, Franz Werfel, and Lion Feuchtwanger tried to improve their fortunes by writing historical novels, considered by Americans a distinguished branch of German literature since the 19th century. Thomas Mann, Heinrich's brother, was most successful winning recognition with his Goethe-novel *Lotte in Weimar*,—a title that needed no translation into English. Thomas Mann had moved from Princeton to Pacific Palisades in 1941 to become "the emperor of all German emigrants, especially the patron saint of the tribe of writers" as the historian of literature Ludwig Marcuse remembered. Mann acted as the father figure for the émigré intellectuals on the West Coast just as Albert Einstein, the other Nobel prize winner in their group, became the representative of the scientists and speaker for the refugees' plight in the East.

The wide range of the émigrés' personalities and of their ideological convictions was bound to cause friction among them, as between the novelist Thomas Mann and Bertolt Brecht, the dramatist. On the other hand, their common fate brought forth similar attitudes. Mann and Brecht shared a certain aloofness from the country of their refuge, and they continued to write in their old language and their accustomed style. For men of letters like Pastorius or Lieber, emigration meant a point of no return; they became and remained Americans. Most of the famous authors who fled to America in the 1930's spent the rest of their lives in a German-speaking country after 1945 when the Hitler nightmare had ended.

America's Schoolteachers

The émigré writers of modern times tried to return, as soon as they could, to the source of their inspiration: the living and changing German language. The teachers among the emigrants from Nazi Germany usually stayed in the United States for good and taught ever more fluently in English.

Pastorius is the earliest example of the German teacher in America who assimilated fast linguistically. We know from a letter to his sons that Pastorius' efforts as a teacher of language began at home. He wrote: "Dear Children, John Samuel and Henry Pastorius: Though you are (Germano sanguine nati) of High Dutch Parents, yet remember that your father was Naturalized, and ye born in an English Colony. Consequently each of you Anglus Natus an Englishman by Birth. Therefore, it would be a shame for you if you should be ignorant of the English Tongue, the Tongue of your Countrymen: but that you may learn the better I have left a Book for you both, and commend the same to your reiterated perusal . . . "

A copy of Pastorius' *New Primmer or Methodical Direction to attain the True Spelling, Reading, and Writing of English*, published in New York in 1698, has survived. In his own catalogue of his works three other textbooks are mentioned to sustain the claim that Pastorius authored the first schoolbooks that originated in America: *Lingua Latina or Grammatical Rudiments*; *Phraseologia Teutonica, Krafft und Safft der Teutschen Helden-Sprach*; and *Lingua Anglicana or some Miscellaneous Remarks concerning the English Language*.

The Quakers in Philadelphia who had provided quality education for their youth in a public school since their arrival were eager to secure Pastorius' services as a teacher of Latin. He left his Germantown home and public offices, and departed for the Friends' School in 1698, where he received a salary of forty pounds per year. His two sons accompanied him to Philadelphia, to their regret. They told their grandfather in Germany about the trials of the eight-hour schoolday in a long letter. The boys only had Saturday afternoons off, and they missed Germantown's "lovely orchards."

Pastorius returned to Germantown after two years, possibly because of a personality clash with a student, and devoted his pedagogical energies to his own group. The instruction of children was mentioned by the settlers from Krefeld as early as 1684, but a full-fledged public school was proposed and opened by Pastorius only by 1701. Alongside his many other duties, Pastorius remained a teacher in Germantown until near the end of his life in 1719. His school was coeducational, and it offered evening instruction for working students. Stressing vocational training, Pastorius urged his students to "learn some respectable practical trade" to serve God and their fellowmen better than by "all scholastic speculation."

Pastorius' skills as a teacher were flawed by occasional outbursts of his "choleric temperament." In the generation after him, gentle Christopher Dock, who taught in a Mennonite school near Germantown, was remembered for letting the laws of kindness rule in the classroom. He introduced the blackboard in American schools. His *Schulordnung*, printed by Christopher Saur in 1750, made Dock a pioneer in American educational theory.

Training in the classics, which Pastorius found useless for Germantown school children, was in demand in the big cities of the post-colonial period. As a teacher of Latin in Philadelphia, Pastorius had set a precedent. The young German scholars who followed in his footsteps usually were professors of theology who taught Latin, Greek, and Hebrew. A pietist school and orphanage in Halle, August Hermann Francke's prestigious Pedagogical Institute, sent many teachers to America.

In the first wave of intellectual emigration from Germany before 1850, some of the revolutionary refugees found ready employment as teachers because of their expertise in the classics. Carl Beck, later a respected professor of Latin language and literature at Harvard University, and his friend Carl Follen, Harvard's first professor of German, were hired by George Bancroft and Joseph Cogswell, who had founded the innovative Round Hill School in Northampton, Massachusetts in 1823. Here they put to the test the experience which they had brought back from studies at the University of Göttingen, and in Pestalozzi's experimental school in Switzerland.

Beck and Follen, together with Franz Lieber, established a new field of schooling in America outside their academic disciplines when they became the founding fathers of physical education. As they transplanted the *Turner* movement from the wars of liberation against Napoleon to America, they did more than revive Juvenal's ancient ideal of cultivating a healthy mind in a healthy body. They set up physical training fields on school grounds, and introduced gymnastics and swimming, but they also spread a message of liberal thought and social progress.

With the influx of like-minded 1848ers, the *Turners'* credo was established in all centers of German-American settlement in newly founded athletic clubs, the *Turnvereine*. Their members, the *Turner*, were influential enough to dominate at times Milwaukee's city politics.

When the outcome of the Civil War satisfied their striving for abolition, the *Turner* concentrated their ideological efforts on education as the cure for social ills. They demanded compulsory school attendance and vocational training. Their leader George Brosius, a house painter and academic self-made man, was appointed Superintendent of Physical Training for the public schools of Milwaukee in 1875.

The athletic associations lost their popularity to spectator sports in the 20th century. The former *Turner* now drew much satisfaction from the remarkable success of the German-Americans as sports stars. Rising out of the anonymity of poor immigrant families to national fame, they appeared as the American dream come true. German-American baseball stars especially lent themselves to hero-worship. Herman, nicknamed "German" Schaeffer, the legendary pinch hitter of the Detroit Tigers, and the Pennsylvania German John Peter (Honus) Wagner who set all-time batting records for the Pittsburgh Pirates, were overshadowed by the stars of the New York Yankees, Lou Gehrig and the unforgettable Babe Ruth. George Herman Ruth, an orphan from the poor Baltimore immigrant family of the Erhardts, became the "Sultan of Swat," the king of kings in a sport that was saturated with half-German slang words like "swatfest," and "bush-leaguer."

Even though the German-American athletic clubs, the *Turnvereine*, changed in their orientation to social, cultural and educational services combined with family-style gymnastic exercise, they by no means ceased to exist. Like the *Männerchöre*, the singing societies, the old *Turnvereine* continue at present to hold on to a proud tradition of American ethnic life and to lend their support to "German Days."

Of all the educational impulses which the 1848ers brought to America, their institution of the kindergarten was more distinctly remembered under its German name than their promotion of physical education and of vocational training. Among Friedrich Froebel's theories which found resonance among American educators from the time of Horace Mann to John Dewey, the idea of children growing like flowers in a garden of creative play proved most popular. Margarethe Meyer Schurz, wife of the statesman Carl Schurz, and Caroline Louise Frankenberg, who had studied with Froebel, were America's first kindergarten teachers in Watertown, Wisconsin, and Columbus, Ohio.

A generation after Froebel, another important innovation, this time in higher education, reached the United

States from Germany. In the creation of the graduate school the experiences of thousands of American professors who had studied in Germany were reflected.

Benjamin Franklin had discovered the scholarly virtues of the University of Göttingen in 1766. The reforms of Wilhelm von Humboldt had made Berlin Europe's most modern university in 1810. It attracted half of the approximately 10,000 American students who studied in Germany before World War I. Heidelberg, another favorite, became a popular symbol of the romantic aspects of Old World studies through its image as the city of the fictional "Student Prince."

The academic influences of American scholars preferring Göttingen, Berlin, and Heidelberg over Oxford and Cambridge became apparent when Johns Hopkins University was founded in 1876. In the same year, the classicist Basil L. Gildersleeve instituted a graduate department in the German pattern of the union of teaching and research. Although he warned of the German tendency toward overspecialization, Gildersleeve's graduate program soon became the model for advanced education in all other major American universities.

At Cornell, President Andrew White set up humanistic and technical-scientific studies side by side, combining the scholarly traditions of a university like Heidelberg with the pragmatic approach of German technical and agricultural universities at Berlin and Hohenheim. Such ties have proved to be binding for over a century. Cornell and Heidelberg still have an exchange program of the kind that links many American institutions of higher education directly with a German partner.

Another president of Cornell University, who like Andrew White became ambassador to Germany, presented the University of Heidelberg with a valuable gift in 1928. Dr. Jacob Gould Schurman had raised over half a million dollars for the much needed New University building from private sources. John D. Rockefeller, whose father had erected a monument for his ancestor from Germany, Johann Peter Rockefeller, in 1906, contributed half of the fund. Most of the rest of this "thanks offering," as Schurman called it, was given by distinguished German-Jewish and Pennsylvania-German donors.

Only a few years after the dedication of Heidelberg's New University, the darkest hour in American-German academic relations approached with Hitler's rise to power. The monumental effects of the exodus of German scholars to America after 1933 still defy an adequate account because of the magnitude and multiformity of their group. The change of countries by Einstein, a genius who distilled the essence of an era into a scientific formula, would by itself be a historical event. But Einstein was only the first among many equals. Brilliant minds tend to outshine each other in the enumeration of famous names representing the "Cultural Migration." Reputations of individuals can fade with time. They can also appear in bright focus if new publications —like Elizabeth Young Bruehl's biography of the political philosopher Hannah Arendt in 1982—elevate a life's work from contemporary discussion to historic significance. The group that was composed of these outstanding individuals has by now secured an uncontested place as one of the major cross-fertilizing intellectual migrations in the history of Western Civilization, often compared to the westward flight of the Greek Byzantine scholars in the fifteenth century.

It has been estimated that more than half of the 7,622 professionals from Germany and Austria who emigrated to the United States in the 1930's were Jewish. The majority were physicians, absorbed with relative ease in private practice. Yet a number of them became professors of medicine. They swelled the ranks of the second-largest and most representative group, the 1,090 teachers. The 1848ers' characteristic occupation was journalism; the members of the "Cultural Migration" in the next century were teacher-scholars in the continental tradition. Politicians and lawyers among the émigrés joined professors of established renown in the arts and sciences in the Institute for Advanced Study in Princeton, the New School for Social Research in New York, and the University of Chicago. At the Princeton Institute, the physicists Einstein and Oppenheimer raised nuclear research to historic importance. In New York, Director Alvin Johnson reorganized his New School for Social Research in 1933 as the "University in Exile." By 1940, sixty émigré scholars taught at what was popularly known as "Little Heidelberg on 12th Street." Economics and Law flourished here besides the three social sciences which had been banned by Hitler: sociology, political science, and psychology. A refuge and gathering point, a unique place of exchange for American and European thought, the New School also served as a stepping stone for the men and women who spread their teaching talent over colleges and universities in every part of the United States.

The scholars of the "Cultural Migration" contributed fresh ideas to established fields. But they also did pioneer work developing newer disciplines like musicology and history of art. Erwin Panofsky from the University of Hamburg had been attracted to the United States by the "Golden Age" of magnificent collections in Princeton and Harvard between 1923 and 1933. In 1934 he was appointed Dean of the Institute of Advanced Studies. He asserted that "history of art's native tongue is German" but praised the liberating effect of his move to America, away from German academic provincialism.

In the long history of German immigration, Germany's loss had never been so clearly America's gain as in the exodus of great teachers in the 1930's. But this loss was compensated. Although the interpretation of the émigrés' cultural roots in the German-speaking countries was spiced with varying degrees of controversy and bitterness, it sparked wide-spread interest, and it raised the level of informed appraisal of the German intellectual heritage. After the war, émigré scholars joined the efforts of drawing up the Federal Republic's Basic Law. The involvement of experts versed both in German and American constitutional law continued a tradition of historical links between the constitutions of both countries: the Basic Law drew on features of the first German democratic constitution that was read in the Frankfurt Paulskirche Assembly during the revolution of 1848/49. The draftsmen of the Paulskirche constitution had in turn been influenced by the ideals and the federal spirit of the American Constitution of 1789.

When West German universities reopened in the late 1940's, many émigrés helped German professors and students to overcome the after-effects of academic isolation caused by totalitarianism. With the aid of the émigrés' books and articles, of their guest lectures and guest professorships, and in some cases their remigration, international dialogue with the German universities was resumed in a remarkably brief time. The endowment of a Theodor Heuss Chair at the New School of Social Research by the Government of the Federal Republic of Germany in 1976, the Bicentennial Year, gave symbolic recognition to the services of the "University in Exile."

Most émigré scholars have retired by now. They have left a void that tends to be filled by ignorance and indifference towards European topics, once enlivened for the previous generation by firsthand experience. The legacy of the "Cultural Migration" has found new advocates in a few outstanding representatives of a second generation, in the double sense of a teacher's biological and intellectual progeny. Among them, Fritz Stern now holds a chair at Columbia University. The promise of the young historian Klaus Epstein was ended by a tragic accident. Hanna Holborn Gray, a historian like her father Hajo Holborn and her aunt Louise W. Holborn, was elected President of the University of Chicago in 1977. Henry Kissinger, son of an émigré teacher from Fürth, was called to Washington from his professorship in Harvard as National Security Advisor, and later became the first German-born U. S. Secretary of State in 1973.

Men of God
in American Churches

In the preface to his account of Pennsylvania in 1692, Pastorius explained the religious motivation of his emigration: "I reasoned thus with myself, whether it were not better to teach the learning which I had received by grace from the highest Giver and Father of Lights to the new-found American peoples of Pennsylvania and thus make them partakers of the true knowledge of the Holy Trinity and true Christianity." Pastorius stuck to his resolution. In the midst of his worldly services for Germantown's pioneers, he remained a missionary, to both Indians and transplanted Europeans. The strong attachment of Pastorius to the Christian religion, the manifold associations in his life with a variety of churches, and his advocacy of the separation of church and state, make the Germantown leader representative of the essence of the German immigration also in spiritual matters.

A distinguishing feature of the German immigration was the diversity of the immigrants' denominational background. The English and the Scots, the Dutch and the Scandinavians were predominantly Protestants; the Irish, the Italians, and the Poles were Catholics. Such a clear-cut identification with a church that strengthened their ethnic self-consciousness was denied to the Germans. The early immigrants, belonging to a wide range of protestant sects, were followed by members of the established Protestant churches, the Lutherans and the Reformed, but also by German Methodist and Baptist groups. In the 19th century, large numbers of Catholics and Jews, and a small but much noticed contingent of Freethinkers completed the denominational heterogeneity of the Germans.

In Pastorius' personal experience, the impact of two churches and three sects blended with surprising harmony. As a young Catholic boy, his father Melchior had suffered grievously at the hands of Lutheran Swedish soldiers in Magdeburg. He married a devout Lutheran, and converted to Lutheranism himself. Francis Daniel Pastorius was raised in his mother's Lutheran faith, but found religious fulfillment in the company of Dr. Spener's Pietist circle in Frankfurt among men and women "who have oil in their lamps and are ready to meet this blessed bridegroom."

Pastorius' own satisfaction with a revivalist movement predestined him for flexible and friendly interaction with congenial sects in Pennsylvania: the Mennonites, and the English, German, and Dutch Quakers. We know that he attended the Quakers' meetings from 1690 on and often served as their recorder. He was open-minded also towards the Indians' beliefs which he called "monotheistic" and "evidently sincere."

The theologian Heinrich Melchior Mühlenberg, the leader of the Lutherans, was a match in organizational and diplomatic talent for the lawyer Pastorius. Beginning in 1742, Mühlenberg tied together isolated and confused congregations "like a modern St. Paul" on his long travels all over the East Coast. By 1765, he had made Dutch, German, and Swedish pastors work together in a number of synods. The Zion Church, a historical gathering place in Philadelphia where Congress held the funeral services for George Washington, was consecrated under his aegis in 1769.

Mühlenberg was a tough frontiersman who pulled himself and his horse out of the ice of Perkiomen Creek close to his home near Philadelphia in the middle of the night. He remained nevertheless a concerned scholar. In contrast to the sectarians who had no mother church in the old country, he could draw strength from continued contacts with his alma mater, the University of Halle, the Protestant theological and educational center that enjoyed American respect for more than a century. Mühlenberg sent all three of his sons to study at Halle. The oldest became a general in the Continental army, the second a member of the Continental Congress and the first Speaker of the United States House of Representatives. The third, a botanist, was the "Principal" of the school that became Franklin and Marshall College.

From Pastorius' arrival until the 19th century, German immigrants were almost exclusively Protestants. Queen Anne had sent the few Catholics among the Palatine emigrants back to the Rhineland. She preferred as settlers prospective pillars of the leading Protestant element in her colonies. Altogether, the sympathies which the Germans on both sides of the Atlantic enjoyed in the United States until 1871 were to a great extent founded on friendly associations with the "Land of Luther."

When the early immigration of small, homogeneous groups of Germans ended, and heterogeneous mass immigration reached the United States by the middle of the 19th century, the Calvinist Reformed Palatines and the Lutheran Württembergers were joined in increasing number by Catholics from Baden, from Bavaria, and from the industrial districts of the Rhineland and Westphalia.

Between 1850 and 1860, the German element in America's foreign born population rose from 26% to 31%. The change of status of the Catholic church from the oldest, but one of the smallest churches to the largest denomination in America began with the Irish mass migration in 1820. It was completed by the end of the century when the new German immigration peaked in the 1880's with a large Catholic contingent. Since this time, the Germans in America have been evenly balanced between Protestants and Catholics.

Rome acknowledged the new importance of the German Catholics in America by appointing a native of Switzerland, Johann Martin Henni, Bishop of Milwaukee in 1844. A generation later, in 1875, Archbishop Henni could look back on the erection of a cathedral, of hospitals, orphanages, schools, and seminaries. Responding to ethnic jealousies of his time, Henni tried to change the traditional pattern of predominantly Irish bishops in the "German triangle of the West", in the archepiscopal sees of Milwaukee, Cincinnati, and St. Louis. The Germans were reminded, however, that they still enjoyed better representation in the Catholic hierarchy than in the U. S. national or state legislatures. In 1918, after the anti-German frenzy of the war had decided the issue in favor of the Irish once and for all, the *Dublin Review* stated categorically: "The Germans are a pillar of the Church in America, but the Irish have always held the rooftop."

Lutherans of German extraction were hit especially hard in 1917 by the hostility of the war years. German-language church services were disrupted. Pastors were threatened as traitors, mainly in the Midwest where the Missouri Synod had been vocal in opposing America's entry into the war. After steering through new anti-German storms in the Second World War, the ethnic ties of church congregations became even more brittle. Yet in Germany's most shameful hour, when the humane and charitable ideals of the Christian-Judaic heritage were trampled down by Nazi boots, a few voices of German theologians were heard in America and understood as a message from the "other Germany." Paul Tillich, the founder of German "religious Socialism" before 1933, came to America at the invitation of Reinhold Niebuhr. He proudly introduced himself: "I had the honor of being the first non-Jewish professor to be expelled from a German university." Dietrich Bonhoeffer spurned the safety of a brief American shelter and returned to martyrdom in Germany. The poetic expression of his unconventional piety caught the ear of the American postwar college generation. Bonhoeffer's *Sonnets from Prison* found many American readers.

Over the centuries, America had served the whole spectrum of spiritual dissent as a refuge for the revivalist and the conservative believer, but also for the non-believer in his alienation from a church-oriented society. In the 19th century, freethinkers from Germany had a lasting impact on the American denominational scene. The philosophical school of the Transcendentalists in New England welcomed the arrival of new liberal theological ideas with some of the 1848ers. The incorporation of their ideas aided the process which led to the founding of the Unitarian Church.

Other thinkers, especially the Socialist Turner, went far beyond the liberal innovations of Unitarianism and promoted a wave of anticlerical agitation. They were bound to clash most violently with the nativist animosities of the "Know-Nothing" movement in the Midwest. These "hair-lipped, red Republican Germans" invited trouble when they asked for direct popular election of all public officials, and for social welfare legislation, when they doubted the constitutional legitimacy of school prayer and of the "Blue Laws" which denied them their beer on Sunday picnics.

The instrinsic value of ingrained traditions in social policy and in the established forms of worship were not only questioned within the Christian churches. Many of the 1848ers were Jews. They added an intellectual element to the laborers and tradesmen who formed the core of the large German-Jewish immigration between 1840 and 1880, and who frequently rose from modest beginnings to great material and cultural wealth. Founders of empires in banking, department stores, and the press, like Solomon Loeb, Jacob H. Schiff, Benjamin Altman, Julius Rosenwald, Otto H. Kahn, and Adolph S. Ochs, arrived in the early 1850's. The Jewish professionals who came to America during the same period excelled as physicians and university teachers. In humanitarian concern and social responsibility, Dr. Abraham Jacobi, a life-long friend of Carl Schurz, was a model of the revolutionaries' credo in action. "The father of American pediatrics" was born in Westphalia. He began on New York's Howard Street, treating poor patients for 25 cents, and topped his career as president of the American Medical Association.

Dr. Jacobi, a highly respected self-made man, was a generation ahead of the socially and financially established German Jews who won distinction as sons of immigrants, like the Frankfurters and Morgenthaus. They dedicated their fortunes to philanthropy and their energies to public service.

In religious life, German-Jewish religious leaders were seeking reforms parallel to the goals of liberal thought introduced by the refugees of the 1830 uprisings. The rabbis who were born and educated in Germany wanted to modernize orthodox Jewry and to bring it closer to the burgeoning century of science. When Rabbi David Einhorn linked the concept of Reform Judaism to the German spirit, traditionalists derided it as the "Jewish Protestant Church." The Reformers countered, calling the orthodox "Finsterlinge"—those who refuse to see the light. Their movement spread fast. Even before the first German-Jewish congregation in Boston was founded in 1843, a Jewish reform society was organized in Baltimore in 1842. Cincinnati became a major center of Jewish reform ideas with its Hebrew Union College, directed by Rabbi Isaac Mayer Wise and his successor Dr. Kaufmann Kohler. Both were trained in German liberal thought. They combined the instruction of rabbis in the Hebrew tradition with the best that contemporary philosophy and science had to offer.

The first Jewish lodge in America added the education of new Jewish immigrants to its social and charitable purposes. The Independent Order of B'nai B'rith, the Sons of the Covenant, was established in New York in 1843. It was originally founded under the name of *Bundes Brüder*, and its ritual was in German.

The predominant cultural and philosophical affinity of the American-Jewish community with Germany changed at the turn of the century when the immigration of over three million Jews from Eastern Europe added different languages and trends. A generation before Hitler unleashed fanatic antisemitism and turned old affection to hate, Jewish solidarity with German interests was still strong enough to be a political factor. In 1917, influential German-Jewish leaders joined forces with spokesmen of the Irish in their efforts to keep America out of the war against Germany.

The centers of the German-Jewish theological heritage which had developed a branch on American soil in the 19th century were destroyed systematically in Germany between 1933 and 1945. Recently a modest beginning was made to create a nucleus of reconstruction for the spiritual traditions of Judaism in Germany. A newly founded Academy of Jewish Studies, associated with the University of Heidelberg, moved into its own building in 1981. Similar to the Leo Baeck Institute in New York, it serves as a center of documentation for the German-Jewish heritage. The Academy's teaching staff offers courses and seminars. Its director, an American, receives triple support for his school from the United States, Israel, and the Federal Republic of Germany. The Academy's library of German Judaica, collected from rescued materials, is growing steadily.

Two characteristics are common to the wide range of different religious beliefs that came to America from Germany: their urgent support of the separation of church and state, and their persistent longevity. Protestant, Catholic, and Jewish Reformed congregations with German roots still exist all over the United States. Even more astonishing is the continued flourishing of the old German sects.

The American branches of the Moravian Brethren are upholding their ideas in a modernized framework. The "plain" Dutch, as the sectarians were called in contrast to the "gay" church people, are by no means less visible in contemporary society. Mennonites, descendants and heirs of the first settlers in 1683, still thrive on model farms. Hutterites stick to their old patterns of communal living almost a century after flourishing Christian communist groups in the countryside near the Ohio River, like the Children of Zoar or the followers of George Rapp in the Harmonist Society, were decimated by their rules of celibacy and by merging with the outside world. The Old Order Amish Mennonites gain in numbers in parts of Pennsylvania, and in the Midwest. Traffic signs alerting the motorist to horses and buggies are seen more frequently in rural America. With families of 17th century proportions, the Amish supply a steady flow of young farmers who seek to buy or rent deserted farms.

Run-down places are restored to viable agricultural enterprises in astounding cooperative endeavors. With help from their relatives, the Amish can still raise a barn in a day, to the surprise of their neighbors whom they call "the English," as in colonial times.

The Amish have hardly changed their dress and their language since their arrival in 1728. They speak a German dialect of the Palatinate with an admixture of the Swiss of their founder Jakob Amman, and some English vocabulary. Their vernacular language is more difficult to understand for a native German than Yiddish, the language of East European Jewish immigrants which resembles the German spoken in Frankfurt in the late Middle Ages. It also reflects the linguistic impact of a group's wanderings. As Hebrew exists side by side with Yiddish as the sacred language of traditionalist Jews, High German is familiar to the Amish only through its use in their worship.

The Amish life-style serves as a reminder of the pre-industrial past of our civilization. Young people are watching it also as a thought-provoking alternative for the future. The growth of the Amish population does not threaten the environment. They use no electricity, and consume oil only for their lamps. They accept an intermediate technology operated not with motors but with their hands. Employment is not their problem. They work from sunrise to sunset, but wisely set aside plenty of time for enjoyment of God's gifts in food and drink, and of each other's company.

Reluctant Involvement
in Politics

Francis Daniel Pastorius' administrative and political abilities were recognized beyond Germantown. He was elected to the provincial legislature and appointed Justice of the Peace in Philadelphia county. He served his hometown as burgomaster, municipal Justice of the Peace, town clerk, tax collector, and councilman. Yet Pastorius did not try to concentrate all authority in his person. On the contrary, he was facing a burdensome necessity. He was deeply disappointed with the citizens of Germantown who were not ready for the municipal self-government which Pastorius knew from the Free Imperial City of Frankfurt.

The men from Krefeld hid behind the Mennonite rules which made them ineligible for election to office. Germantown's preoccupation with their "quiet, godly life" permitted hardly more than a sigh of relief when the city's charter of self-rule was suspended in 1707. After all, the townspeople took comfort, they would now save the municipal taxes. In 1703 Pastorius complained bitterly to William Penn about the unwillingness of his townsfolk to share his administrative burdens. His hope that future immigrants from Germany would bring leadership to America was to be fulfilled only when the émigrés after 1848 and 1933 sought and found political freedom in the United States.

In colonial times, the assertiveness and gift for leadership displayed by the English and Scotch-Irish made the Germans appear all the more politically withdrawn. When mass migration from Ireland and Germany changed the ethnic composition of the population in the 19th century, German-American political apathy again compared unfavorably with the lively and successful engagement of the Irish in domestic politics. The Germans first appeared in the political arena to defend their old-world life-style against xenophobic attacks of the nativist Know-Nothing movement in the campaigns of 1856 and 1860. All of their factions rallied behind the slogan "Liberty and Lagerbier" which the Republican Party aimed at its large German constituency. Yet the German-American electorate was divided into a sizable body of followers, and a thin layer of leaders. To the average immigrant, the émigrés of the German revolutions were suspect as radical eggheads. The

1848ers criticized the rank and file of the German-Americans as too conservative, conformist, law-and-order oriented, and tied to narrow horizons of overriding concern with material betterment offered by the "land of boundless opportunities." Julius Froebel, an émigré and nephew of Friedrich Froebel, called the German-Americans *Stimmvieh*, undiscerning voters flocking to the polls like cattle to their trough.

Similar mutual disapproval divided old-timers and newcomers after the arrival of the émigrés from Hitler in the 1930's. In spite of their political disinterest, the bulk of the German-American organizations had enough sound judgment to turn their backs on the Nazi agitation which spilled over from Germany in the *Deutschamerikanischer Volksbund*. The small but vociferous group received much publicity until their leader Fritz Kuhn was convicted for embezzlement in 1939.

Lack of active political involvement is cited to this day as a characteristic of the German-descended element wherever it is still distinguishable from the Anglo-Saxon mainstream. The traits considered as typically German have merged with the qualities of America's contemporary "silent majority." The 28% of Americans who claimed German ancestry in 1982 remain inconspicuous in their assuredness that they belong to the core of the American people and can afford to live with a low profile.

Aware of their shortcomings in political activities, German-Americans traditionally have taken heart looking upon Carl Schurz for inspiration. Schurz was a president-maker who led hundreds of thousands of German-Americans into the Republican camp with his eloquence in 1860. "No man is closer to my heart than you are," Abraham Lincoln told him. During the Civil War, Schurz combined courage with shrewd political calculation in his effort to swing the cautious president toward a more decisive stance proclaiming the freedom of the slaves in the southern states. When Schurz asked Lincoln for a recall from his recent appointment as Minister to Spain and wished to be given a field command, he could invoke European public opinion in support of his own strong convictions in favor of abolition.

As a U. S. Senator from Missouri in 1869, Schurz began to work against corruption and the spoils system. His appointment as Secretary of the Interior under President Hayes gave him a platform for introducing the merit system for holders of public office. In other ways, too, he followed the spirit of his own rewording of "my country, right or wrong," into: "if wrong, to be set right." He imported his native country's high regard for forests and their systematic, scientific care. The wasteful denuding of American forest land by lumber barons hurt him deeply. When he implemented a carefully planned program of reforestation, he became a forerunner of 20th century principles of conservation.

The Republican Schurz' endeavors to extend the benefits of America's largesse to the Blacks and the Indians were complemented by John Peter Altgeld as a politician "who served the wretched, the deprived, the lame, and the poor." Altgeld had arrived from Hesse as the infant son of an illiterate laborer. He worked his way through law school and managed, to general surprise, to be elected Governor of Illinois on a platform combining the Democrats and the United Labor Party. His attempts to prohibit child labor and to improve sanitary conditions in factories produced both admirers and enemies. As governor, he did not shrink from jeopardizing his further career by pardoning three anarchists when he recognized that they were unjustly imprisoned in conjunction with the Haymarket bombing in Chicago on May 4, 1886.

In the 1880's, another small group of political refugees, this time from Bismarck's suppression of the German Social Democratic Party, reinforced the ranks of German immigrants with socially progressive aspirations. One of them, Charles Proteus Steinmetz, kept up his propagation of socialist ideas in the American Socialist Party. He had fled from trouble in his student days at the University of Breslau in Silesia. He continued his political lectures after his inventions in electrical engineering had earned him the title "Wizard of Schenectady" and a crucial position in the development of the General Electric company.

The German-American support of socialism, the labor movement and the first unions carried over into the 20th century. The background of U. S. Senator Robert Wagner of New York resembled Altgeld's origins. He also immigrated from Germany as a child, supported himself through law school, and became a champion of the underprivileged. The National Labor Relations Act of 1935 is known as the Wagner Act.

Wagner was involved in all other aspects of the 1930s' social legislation as well, from the Relief Act for the Unemployed in 1932 to the first introduction of a national health insurance bill in 1939. He co-authored the Social Security Act of 1935 and became "indissolubly tied," as President Franklin D. Roosevelt said, to "America's second Bill of Rights."

The German Labor Movement had come from Europe to America with the exodus of the socialist "Turners." A century later, in the mid-1950's, American labor unions took the initiative in forging new links with their counterparts in Germany. This was the time when Walter Reuther, the German-American chairman of the United Auto Workers, and instrumental in the merger of the AFL-CIO, established easy rapport with his colleagues in West Germany.

German-American legislators and union leaders were noticed all the more because there were so few of them, considering the numbers of their group which had grown by over 5 million immigrants in the 19th century alone. Yet the weak voice of the Germans in politics was amplified by masters in the shaping of public opinion like Thomas Nast, the illustrator, an 1848er refugee and son of a trombone player in the Palatinate. Through the medium of his cartoons, Nast reinforced the work of Carl Schurz in many respects. He also was recognized as a "president maker," and was appreciated by Abraham Lincoln as "our best recruiting sergeant." Nast fought for human rights of minorities, including the newly arrived Chinese. He attacked corruption with his pen drawings in *Harper's Weekly*, and invented emblems like the aggressive and rapacious tiger, standing for Tammany Hall, the organization of Boss Tweed in New York's city government. Boss Tweed tried to fight back with threats, bribes, and with denunciations in the press of the "Nast-y artist of Harper's Hell Weekly." Nast prevailed, Boss Tweed landed in jail, and the cartoonist became a celebrity. His niche in the lore of American politics was secured in the election campaign of 1874 when Nast introduced the elephant as the symbol of the Republican Party. The corresponding, already existing symbol, the Democrats' donkey, became firmly established in the process.

Nast's figures enjoyed tremendous popularity, from Uncle Sam and John Bull to his friendly self-portraits as Santa Claus, a childhood memory of the "pelzenickels," the small bearded creatures of pre-Christmas folk customs in his native Palatinate. But he was no businessman, and his financial fortunes declined swiftly in the 1890's. President Theodore Roosevelt, an old fan, observed: "I owe my first lesson in practical politics to Thomas Nast." Yet he did the cartoonist a poor service by appointing him consul to Ecuador, where Nast died in the tropical climate of yellow fever at the age of sixty-two.

Nast's illustrative art made the cartoon a power in politics. The heritage of his style can be traced also in journalistic entertainment. It is closely related to the drawings of his contemporary Wilhelm Busch, the master of humorous picture stories. When William Randolph Hearst's *Sunday Journal* commissioned its German-born illustrator Rudolf Dirks to boost circulation by an imitation of Wilhelm Busch's *Max and Moritz* series, the American comic strip was born with Hans and Fritz, the *Katzenjammer Kids*.

Pacifists and Soldiers

Carl Schurz fought for his political ideals also on battlefields as a Major General. In the Civil War as in the War of Independence, the Germans provided officers and soldiers. They were not, however, regarded as born warriors. On the contrary, they had introduced themselves as determined pacifists in the first waves of their immigration.

In his farewell letter to his father, Pastorius mentioned his satisfaction at escaping Europe's wars and unrest. He was looking above all for a peaceful life. The settlers from Krefeld were mostly Mennonites who "rejected all arms, except the sword of the Spirit." The spectre of conscription had driven the members of many German sects out of their native land. For these pacifists, the English Quakers' stand against military force had been a major attraction. As conscientious objectors, Zinzendorf's Moravian Brethren had moved from Georgia to Pennsylvania. In North Carolina, they were exempted from military service but paid for the privilege with a triple tax, not counting scorn and derision by their Irish neighbors.

George Washington appreciated the Moravians' service without arms as good Samaritans for his hard-pressed troops. In the same supportive spirit the Dunkers at Ephrata Cloister turned their schoolhouse into an army hospital after the battle of Brandywine.

Unlike the adherents of pacifist sects, the German church people were fighters. Henry Muhlenberg's oldest son John Peter Gabriel became their idol. His career as a young minister in Woodstock, Virginia, ended with a dramatic service in January, 1776. He closed the appeal to his congregation to revolt against oppression with the words: "There is a time for preaching and praying, but there is also a time for battle, and that time has now arrived." Shedding his clerical robe, he walked away in the blue and silver colonel's uniform of the Continental Army, and took over his fast growing German-American regiment.

German military units were formed in Pennsylvania, in Maryland, in Virginia, and as far south as Charleston. The dedicated German generals became important symbols for the German-American community's ethnic identity. They proved that the Germans in America also provided leaders.

The inhabitants of the "German Flats" in the fertile farming region of the Mohawk Valley in New York State formed four batallions in 1775 under the command of Nikolas Herkimer. They later renamed their major settlement "Herkimer" in memory of the general who died of wounds from the Battle of Oriskany where George Washington credited Herkimer with the reversal of "the gloomy scene."

Counties in several states are named for the Bavarian Johann de Kalb, another general who gave his life for the cause of the Revolution in the lost battle of Camden in South Carolina. The Marquis de Lafayette, whose services for the War of Independence de Kalb had secured, laid the cornerstone for the monument in Camden that was dedicated to de Kalb, "German by birth, cosmopolitan by principle." He served "the fight for independence out of his love for freedom."

Baron Friedrich Wilhelm von Steuben was Washington's most valuable and most lastingly appreciated military assistant. The organizer and administrator of the Revolutionary Army came from Prussia and had served under Frederick the Great.

When he joined Washington's winter quarters at Valley Forge, Steuben set a new precedent. As a Major General, he drilled the decimated and demoralized troops himself. He respected them as patriotic volunteers in need of systematic training. He dealt with his linguistic difficulties when he ran out of German and French by calling on his adjutant: "My dear Walker, come and swear for me in English." His swearing was perfunctory. In his manual of Army regulations, the "Blue Book," he asked officers to treat their men "with all possible friendship and humanity," and to give reasons for their commands.

Efficiency and frugality were stressed as soldierly virtues. After one year of Steuben's service as Inspector General, the War Office found only three muskets missing instead of the customary loss of five to eight thousand. After long hesitation, George Washington finally entrusted Steuben with the command of front-line troops at the battle of Yorktown in 1781. There Steuben was the first to learn that emmissaries of the British commander Cornwallis were approaching with a white flag, announcing negotiations for surrender.

The gratitude of his country reached Steuben in word and deed. President Washington addressed his last letter in office to the Baron as a "farewell token of my sincere friendship and esteem," and "to express my sense of the obligations the public is under to you for your faithful and meritorious services." Counties, cities, and individuals took his name. Steuben was voted over 30,000 acres of unsettled land, more than half of it by the state of New York. The Baron liked to spend money only too well, but later also used his wealth in support of associations aiding poor immigrants.

Steuben's name and prestige were invoked in 1919. In an effort to rebuild German-American self-confidence from the ravages of the war, the Steuben Society was founded upon the principles of "Duty, Justice, Charity, and Tolerance." After World War II, Steuben Societies in Frankfurt and other West German cities encouraged social contacts between Americans on overseas duty and German citizens.

Far from acknowledgement by kings, presidents, and legislatures, the War of Independence involved the lives of thousands of Germans on both sides. Two folk heroes of the American Revolution are still remembered. Christopher Ludwig, the "honest baker," refused any excessive material gain as director of baking, and was proud of the money which he saved the Continental Army. "Molly Pitcher" actually was named Maria, also a Ludwig. She was the wife of a soldier and joined her wounded husband, William Hayes, in the Revolutionary camp. As a self-styled medic, as a cook for the battery, and in case of emergency as a canoneer, she became a historical legend.

A considerable portion of the Germans whom the King of England had hired as mercenaries for his battles against the American Revolutionaries were destined to become a distinct group of new settlers on American soil. Estimates of the numbers of Hessian soldiers who remained in the United States after the war range from 5,000 to 12,000. In 1776, the Continental Congress began to lure the Hessians from their British commanders by promising them 50 acres of land apiece, and the rights of a native American. The appeal, cleverly circulated on the backs of tobacco wrappers, found resonance among the Hessians, who were not fighting for their own cause, and many a soldier became a farmer within or near a German settlement.

In the Civil War, Germans were again fighting on both sides, but their greatest numbers and their idealistic energies were clearly with the Union armies. The 1848ers were emphatically engaged in the fight against slavery. President Theodore Roosevelt summed up the impact of Schurz and his group when he said in a speech in 1903: " . . . it would be difficult to paint in too strong colors what I may well-nigh call the all-importance of American citizens of German birth and extraction toward the cause of the Union and liberty."

The higher officers of the German contingents were not tactical wizards. As a general, Carl Schurz was still a politician. General Franz Sigel's success in holding Missouri in the Union was contingent on the concerted efforts of the Turner societies and other German groups in St. Louis. The flamboyant and personable Hecker, revered as "Red Friedrich" by 1848ers in Germany and America alike, became the recruiter and commander of the 24th, later the 82nd Illinois regiment. Hecker regarded his military career mainly as an extension of his political involvement in the Republican Party and the election of Lincoln. It represented a break in his life as a "Latin Farmer" near Belleville, Illinois, where he had retreated from the frustrated revolutionary ambitions of his youth. Another German colonel, Gustav Koerner, belonged to the earlier revolutionary refugees of 1830. He worked with Lincoln, and was better remembered as Lt. Governor of Illinois than as a military man.

In spite of all painful political repercussions of the two World Wars for the German-Americans, the allegiance of American soldiers of German descent never was an issue. It was noticed after 1941 that German names were well represented in positions of high command with a Spaatz, a

Nimitz, an Eisenhower. This fact tended to be associated with the stereotype of German military prowess—a relatively new concept that had certainly not originated from observation of the German element in America.

As the name indicates, Dwight David Eisenhower's German ancestors were iron miners. Genealogists agree that they came from the Palatinate near Heidelberg. Reliable evidence is based upon the record that Adam Eisenhauer from Wilhelmsfeld was permitted to emigrate to America in 1751 on payment of the usual taxes, and that he became, with other immigrants from Switzerland and England, a forefather of the president's family.

Early Humanitarian Concern

In the German immigrants' minds, Germany's lack of overseas colonies had produced images of slavery and of people belonging to other races that were quite different from the impressions derived by the English and Dutch settlers from their historical experience. The Germans in America were seldom employers of labor on a large scale. Many of them had experienced the stress of indentured service. Their shock at the practice of importing black men in bondage from the West Indies and later from Africa was not constrained by economic self-interest.

Only four and a half years after the founding of Germantown, its citizens submitted a formal protest against slavery to the Monthly Quaker Meeting of the Province in Dublin, north of Philadelphia. Germantown's statement against slavery was signed on April 18, 1688, by Francis Daniel Pastorius, and three weavers from Mennonite families in Krefeld. It was fitted into two tightly penned pages, in the hand of Pastorius, who expressed similar ideas in two brief, didactic poems. In awkward rhyme, Pastorius promised hellfire if we "transgress Christ's precepts: "Negroes by slavery oppress, And white ones grieve by usury." Pastorius invoked the Golden Rule in agreement with the opening paragraph of the Germantown document. The protesters gave—here in the original spelling—as "reasons why we are against the traffick of mensbody: "Is there any that would be done or handled at this matter? vis. to be sold or made a slave for all the time of his life?" The readers were reminded how "fearfull & fainthearted" they, too, had been in view of the possibility that "they should be taken and sold for Slaves in Turckey" by Turkish corsairs on their journey over the Atlantic. Worse than the Turks, Christians steal black men. They are committing "adultery in others, separating wives from husbands, and giving them to others and some sell children of those poor Creatures to other men."

Anticipating the Declaration of Independence, the citizens of Germantown demanded "that we shall doe to all men, licke as we will be done ourselves, ... making no difference of what generation, descent or Colour they are ... tho' they are black we cannot conceive there is more liberty to have them slaves, as it is to have other white ones." The protesters told their Quaker brothers outright: "Here is liberty of Conscience, whch is right & reasonable; here ought to be lickewise liberty of ye body..." In Europe there are many oppressed for Conscience sacke; and here there are those oppressed wch are of a black Colour."

The pragmatists among the colonial leaders were warned about the economic consequences of their blighted reputation: "This mackes an ill report in all those Countries of Europe, where they hear off, that ye Quakers doe here handel man, Licke they handel there ye Cattel, and for that reason some have no mind or inclination to come hither. And who shall maintaine this your cause or plaid for it!"

The protesters concluded: "therefore we contradict & are against this traffick of men body" and demanded that "such men ought to be delivred out of ye hands of ye Robbers and set free as well as in Europe."

The Quaker meeting at Dublin passed the embarrassing matter on to the next higher level, the Quarterly meeting. It was put to rest at the Yearly meeting having so "General a Relation to many other Parts." Nearly a hundred years later, in 1776, the Quakers of Pennsylvania gave a signal to the country by setting all their slaves free.

In spite of the Quaker meeting's comment on the protest: "...ye tennor of it being nearly Related to ye truth...," the German settlers move was resented and considered, quite literally, as a "holier-than-thou" presumption. Petty unpleasantness followed. The honeymoon of mutual affection between Germantown and Philadelphia was running out.

The protest of the Germantown settlers was followed by similar reactions of German immigrants to conditions which did not measure up to the degree of freedom and justice which they had expected in their new country. Time and again, acting as the self-appointed conscience of their neighbors did not endear the Germans to the powers-that-be. The Salzburg Protestants in Georgia encountered the indignant hostility of local landowners when they insisted that their colony was an asylum for all oppressed, and asked for release of the black slaves. Yet their opportunistic mother church in Augsburg advised moderation, and the Salzburgers' outspoken pastor Boltzius backed down.

Almost a century later, in 1836, the émigré Carl Follen had to suffer the consequences of a more gallant stand. In his *Address to the American People*, and witnessing before the Massachusetts legislature, he vowed: "As long as I live, as a good American, as a good German, and as a good Christian, I will fight for the cause of the liberation of the Negroes." The relatives of Follen's wife Eliza Lee Cabot, among Boston's first families, cooled off in their formerly warm relations with the likable young immigrant scholar when he spoke up as an abolitionist. Follen's outspoken fervor also cost him the renewal of his position as the first Professor of German at Harvard University.

Follen's fiery comrade in arms, Karl Heinzen, has been called a German Thomas Paine. In his periodical, the German-language *Pionier*, Heinzen thundered against the "disease of slavery" that "drains the American Republic's strength."

Carl Schurz carried the 1848ers ideals in their fight for abolition over into the controversies of the Reconstruction period. After the Civil War, he toured the South for President Johnson and wrote an urgent report advocating human rights for the freed Negro slaves.

Consideration for the Indians was demanded by German immigrants side by side with the espousal of human rights for Blacks. Long before Germantown was founded, a special affinity of the Germans for the Red Man was noticed, with strong disapproval. In the troubled Jamestown colony of 1607, German carpenters fraternized with the Indians when they were ordered to build a house for King Powhatan. Captain Smith was furious and labeled them traitors. He let one of the Germans who were caught "go by the heels." The episode is supposed to have prompted him to coin the epithet "Damn Dutch" which became a favorite catchword of the 19th century Nativists who were upset by uncouth, beer-guzzling German immigrants.

The Germantown settlers welcomed William Penn's treaties with the Indians. Pastorius wrote to fascinated friends in Germany: "I was the other day at the table of our Governor William Penn, and met there a King of the savages. William Penn told him that I was a German and came from the lands farthest away. A few days afterwards he came with his Queen to Germantown to see me. I treated them as well as I could with food and drink, where upon he showed a great attachment to me and called me Carissimo, which is brother."

Pastorius, the linguist, was puzzled with the language of the Indians and finally decided it was closest in sound to Italian. He knew the Lenni Lenape Indians well and called them "the not-so savage savages." They came to Germantown not only for the customary sale of their fish and game, but also, in an unusual arrangement, for regular work. Pastorius reported: "In the meantime we use the savage people's services as day laborers, gradually learn their language, and get them to know, by and by, Christ's teachings." The close contact of the settlers with the Indians eventually led to an exchange rate with their currency: Twelve pieces of their brown, and twenty of their white "coral money" were worth one Frankfurt albus.

Long before Rousseau paid homage to the noble savage, Pastorius extolled Indian virtues. He allowed exceptions to the natives' honesty only when they had been spoiled by contacts with Whites. He told about a "very cunning savage" who tried to sell him an eagle, insisting that it was a turkey. Pastorius was not fooled but overheard the Indian say "to a Swede standing by that he had not supposed that a German so lately arrived would know these birds apart."

Repeatedly, Pastorius vents his fury against "the Mouth-Christians, who, for their own profit, sell the cursed strong drink" to the Indians. He expresses his sorrow when he records that three quarters of the aboriginies died of diseases in the decade since he arrived; yet he apparently was not aware of the European origin of their epidemics.

The friendly relations of the Germantown settlers with their Indian neighbors were possibly surpassed by Zinzendorf's Moravian Brethren. The "Herrnhuter" are still committed missionaries to the Indians. In colonial times this association aroused the hostility of other settlers, especially because the missionaires carried it to the point of intermarriage.

Johann Conrad Weiser was a leader of the Palatines who had bought land from the Mohawk Indians in the Schoharie Valley in 1713. Although the close rapport of the settlers with the Indians aroused the animosity of Governor Hunter of New York, Weiser let his young son Conrad grow up with a local Indian tribe. Conrad Weiser's familiarity with Indian culture made his services invaluable in 1737 and 1745 when he acted as a negotiator and peace-maker with the tribes of the Iroquois Nation for the governors of Pennsylvania and Virginia.

In the 19th century, when the Indians had been reduced to a minority, they were still held in high regard by the German-Americans. Co-operative insurance societies of German working men fashioned the organization of a "Red Man's Order" along the lines of Indian lore and called themselves the "German Tribes." Carl Schurz acted as the advocate of the Indians in Washington. The artists of the Düsseldorf School chose them as one of their favorite themes. They preserved their impressions of the Red Man's free life on the prairies in drawings and oils, before it became historical memory.

Joys of the Good and Simple Life

At the center of Germantown's Main Street was an open market in the old-world tradition, serving an economic necessity, and providing social pleasure. Special harvest-time fairs became increasingly popular after 1701. The German fall fairs moved on with the pioneers who passed through Germantown to settlements further west and became a permanent institution in rural America.

The prosperous German artisans and craftsmen in Milwaukee, Cincinnati, and St. Louis lived well. They adopted wholeheartedly Goethe's formula for a fulfilled life: work in the daytime, followed by conviviality in the evening; rough weeks of toil, relieved by festive holidays and merry-making.

The Germans' lighthearted celebration of Sunday initially caused them much distress, yet they eventually won out against their puritanical censors. President John F. Kennedy observed: "To the influence of the German immigrants in particular—although all minority groups contributed—we owe the mellowing of the austere Puritan imprint on our daily lives. The Puritans observed the Sabbath as a day of silence and solemnity. The Germans clung to their concept of the 'continental Sunday' as a day not only of churchgoing, but also of relaxation, of picnics, of visiting, of quiet drinking in beer gardens while listening to the music of a band."

Like the cheerful continental Sunday, the Germans' way to celebrate Christmas and Easter proved irresistible and soon mingled with the traditions of English and Scandinavian Yuletide. Immigrants perpetuated the legend that the Christmas tree had originated in the former monastery at Wittenberg where Martin and Katharina Luther set it up for their children. A historical record of a Christmas tree was established only in 1708, when Princess Elisabeth Charlotte of the Palatinate described a boxwood with a candle on every branch. The tune of *O Tannenbaum*, the traditional song in praise of the Christmas tree, was used for the anthem of the State of Maryland. America was among the first of many countries to adopt "Silent Night" as a favorite Christmas song. It was first heard in the country church of St. Nikolas in Oberndorf, near Salzburg and the Austrian-German border, on Christmas Eve, 1818. Groups of Tyrolean singers took *Silent Night* to Germany, and soon also to the United States.

Singing, eating, and drinking were inseparable parts of festivities. More than the Germans' fancy holiday dishes, their hearty everyday fare became part of the American kitchen. Their meat specialties, linked to the names of German-speaking cities, the hamburgers, frankfurters, and wieners; the endless variety of sausages and cheeses and bakeries; the sauerkraut, apple-butter, and potato salad —all these humble but indispensable treats are too American to be considered ethnic foods.

The solid middle-class preferences of the German immigrants were also reflected in their favorite beverages. As an American institution, the coffee klatch has lost the connotation of "gossip" inherent in the original German term. Contemporary visitors from Germany are often overwhelmed with the prevalence of "beer" as the first American association with "German". The word "beerstein" for the drink's vessel, once brought over by German immigrants, has disappeared from use in Germany and is only familiar to clerks in souvenir shops frequented by American tourists. Native Germans might cringe at the selection of beer as too narrow and prosaic a symbol for German life-style and regret the stereotypes which this cliché reinforces. But the historical role of beer in the emergence of the German-American community is undebatable.

The docile burghers in the Midwest's German Belt first asserted themselves when they pressed for their right to have a beer whenever they pleased. An incident of talking back to authorities in as personal a matter as drink is reported from the first German pub in America in Germantown. Peter Keurlis, the innkeeper, was hauled into court in 1695. He was asked by the judge why he did not abide by the law of Germantown corporation to sell no more than a gill of rum or a quart of beer every half day to each customer. Keurlis replied: "They being able to bear more," he could or would not obey that law.

German vintners made Missouri a major wine-producing state, and Julius Drexel, an 1848er law student, laid out the first Rhine-wine farm in Sonoma county, California. Pastorius had hoped in vain to base one of Germantown's industries upon the grape. But in all phases of the German immigration beer was the essence of cozy conviviality, of *Gemütlichkeit*, in German-American clubs and associations. Beer was the hallmark of their celebrations from the 4th of July to the Oktoberfest, it was the balm, and at times the ruin, of singers' voices in the men's choirs.

Beer also became a major German-American industry. Best, Pabst and Schlitz, "the beer that made Milwaukee famous," enjoyed nationwide distribution by 1860. Eberhard Anheuser, the owner of a Bavarian brewery, and Adolphus Busch from a wine-merchant's family in Mainz produced the popular Budweiser beer in their Anheuser-Busch company in St. Louis by hundreds of thousands of barrels in the 1870's. Beer brewers became patrons of the arts. Adolphus Busch and his son-in-law Hugo Reisinger provided the funds to house the Museum of Germanic Culture which was established at Harvard University in 1903.

Germans were frequently engaged in the processing of food and drink. Many a modest craftsman among the German butchers and bakers, the wine-and-beer makers, became an industrialist as a meat packer or producer of sugar, salt, and yeast on a large scale.

Just as lowly, but also as ubiquitous and affordable as a hamburger and a beer, was a piece of clothing that was introduced by an immigrant from Bavaria who arrived in

1845, one of the numerous German-Jewish clothiers of the 19th century. The story of blue jeans, a symbol of the egalitarian American way of life, is inseparably tied to the travelings of young Levi Strauss. He picked up a supply of canvas before he sailed from New York to San Francisco to join the California gold rush. Levi Strauss did not find gold in prospecting. Rather he discovered a gold mine in the tightly woven canvas, originally intended for covers of the Conestoga wagons manufactured by the Pennsylvania Dutch in Lancaster county. Tailored into pants, the tough material was strong enough to withstand the rigors of gold-mining.

A century after the Strauss Brothers' firm was founded in 1873, "Levis" have lost nothing of their attraction. On the contrary, they have become a hot article for export. In Europe and all over the world they are eagerly sought by young people, whether they are friendly to the jeans' country of origin or not.

Family Ties

Pastorius urged his sons to become wholeheartedly assimilated citizens of the American colonies but he also encouraged them to keep up contact with their grandfather and other relatives in Germany. In 1699, John Samuel and Heinrich Pastorius, nine and seven years old, wrote in a letter to Melchior Pastorius, mayor of Windsheim: "We often wish that we were with thee or that thou lived here in our house in Germantown which has a beautiful front garden... Since we cannot now have the hope that we will see our dear grandfather here with us we pray thee to give us some account of thy origin and our elders. So that if one of us should, by God's will, go to Germany we can ask after our relations. Will thee also give our friendly greeting to our dear cousins and aunts and show them this so that they often write letters to us... and we shall not fail through the help of other pious people to continue the correspondence."

Immigrants writing to relatives back home frequently caused a chain reaction of family-group migration. Historical collections of letters show that the Germans on both sides of the Atlantic communicated persistently. In the jet age, they visit frequently enough to boost the revenue received from tourism both in Germany and the United States.

Like other ethnic groups, the German-American community cared for its needy members. Its prominent representatives provided for indigent newcomers, from the times of Steuben to the 1930's, when the trust set up for the Carl Schurz Memorial Foundation by Gustav Oberlaender, an industrialist born in the Rhineland, was put at the disposal of German refugees. Philanthropists extended a helpful hand also to the mother country in times of emergency. Anna and Oswald Ottendorfer, owners of the *Staats-Zeitung*, sponsored German hospitals in New York and New Jersey, as well as helping flood victims near the Rhine and Vistula rivers in 1882.

President Hoover, a descendant of Andreas Huber who emigrated from the Palatinate in 1738, became the benefactor of malnourished German children after the First and Second World Wars. Two newly-coined verbs in the German language, "quakern" and "hoovern," meaning to eat from American food donations, became a part of school children's vocabulary.

The lean years from 1945 to 1950 revived countless dormant family contacts between cousins and second cousins in the United States and Germany. The rich "uncle from America" who emerged from nowhere, splurging on a visit back home, had been part of German lore for generations. In the post-war gloom of German cities, such legendary, distant but concerned American relatives became substantial as senders of CARE parcels. They often spent more relative to their means than imagined by the recipients overseas, for whom the largesse from "over there" had a miraculous quality. Through the channels of university administrations and churches, hungry students and old people without connections in the United States were included as beneficiaries of American compassion. Five million CARE packages arrived in Germany after the war. Spontaneous, unorganized gifts are estimated to amount to the equivalent of 200 million dollars.

Older West Germans still remember the warmth of this giving. It made as lasting an impression on the man in the street as U.S. Government aid for the newly founded Federal Republic of Germany in form of the Marshall Plan. The German Marshall Fund of the U.S., financed by the West German government, gave official expression to the gratitude of the German people. Yet it proved difficult to hand these memories on to the next generation of young Germans who grew up remote from the personal experience of hard times.

PRESENT-DAY HERITAGE

3

New Life in
Old Organizations

In the 1980's, local memories of Germantown's founding fathers have grown dim. The original homes of the settlers with their slanted roofs, covered with tile or layered oak shingles in old world fashion, have all but disappeared. Street names from Pastorius' day and the name "Germantown" remain in what became the 22nd ward of Philadelphia. Its distinctly German inhabitants dispersed well over a century ago when Germantown became "America's most beautiful suburb." The Irish, and later the Italians prevailed in the 20th century, until Germantown became more recently a part of Philadelphia's Black community.

For the small segment of German-Americans who are still actively involved in ethnic associations, Germantown continues to be a place of pilgrimage. The shimmering white monument in Vernon Park, honoring Pastorius and his settlers, has been a favorite gathering place over the generations. It attracted large crowds on special "Pastorius Days," notably in 1933 and 1958, commemorating the 250th and 275th anniversary of the beginnings of Germantown.

In the academic world, the symbolism of Pastorius' name is matched by Carl Schurz. In popular appeal, Pastorius is surpassed by Steuben whose memory is evoked in the Steuben Parades every year on New York's Fifth Avenue since 1958.

Many of the long-established German clubs have by now passed their hundredth anniversary. The grandchildren of their founders have usually assimilated to a point where their interest in the old associations has dwindled. But a number of new factors has counterbalanced the process of the clubs' disintegration.

When the Bicentennial celebrations in 1976 rekindled curiosity in the American people's roots, the ethnic consciousness of Americans of German descent was reactivated. Genealogical research institutes from the Rhineland to Berlin are swamped with inquiries from the United States. German-Americans are again getting together more frequently for social, musical and sportive events.

A new wave of popularity of America's folkloristic heritage gave a boost to the club-life of associations intent on preserving the traditions of specific regions of the German-speaking countries. At a time when Pennsylvania

Dutch folk art came into vogue, when the bold symmetry of Amish quilts was newly appreciated, the festivals of the Swabians and Bavarians, of the Tyroleans, and the Swiss sharp-shooters enjoyed increasing appeal to the public. The pleasures of German rural merrymaking have captivated America's city dwellers from coast to coast. Oktoberfest celebrations are proliferating. It is fitting indeed that plans for the observation of the Tricentennial of German immigration were not limited to the meeting of Presidents and scholarly symposia at major universities but included a string of popular festivals on both sides of the Atlantic, from the Rhineland to Main Street, U.S.A. Oompah bands, Schuhplattler dances, colorful dirndl costumes, and servings of pretzels, of beer, and sausages represent more than ever a common ground of American and German recreation.

Among the celebrants of the German-American clubs will be a new element. In the decade after 1945, the United States and Canada often proved to be the final destination for Germans uprooted by forced wartime migrations. Many of the 226,578 German immigrants who entered the United States between 1941 and 1950 were admitted under the Displaced Persons Act. There were expellees, trying to move on to the United States, part of the group of ten million homeless people from the eastern parts of prewar Germany that are now Polish and Russian territory. Others belonged to ethnic German groups who had to leave centuries-old enclaves in Eastern Europe, from Czechoslovakia and Rumania to Hungary and Yugoslavia. The contemporary experience of these ''Volksdeutsche'' repeated the Russian-Germans' patterns of migration from the previous century. German Mennonites had preserved their ethnicity in settlements along the Volga River since Catherine the Great had invited them to cultivate the Russian steppe. When they were forced to migrate on to America after 1873, they brought along in large chests an invaluable contribution to the Midwest's agricultural wealth: red hard Turkey winter wheat, perfectly suited for the growing season in Kansas.

Like the Russian-Germans who continued to cling tenaciously to their old language and customs in the Midwest, 20th century immigrants with strong ties to a regional group felt compelled to keep up old affiliations in their new country. German-American associations of the 1950's, composed of Sudeten Germans, East Prussians, or Silesians emerged out of a peculiar historical situation. These groups had not been hurt by the traumatic experience of their older sister organizations which were shaken twice by devastating anti-German sentiment, especially during the First World War. The more recently founded clubs are close in spirit to their counterparts in Italian-American or Polish-American communities. They are interested in keeping in touch with the country of their linguistic and cultural origin, and they want to remain informed. They are concerned about friendly relations between West Germany and their adopted country, and they speak up against the stubborn reappearance of unfair stereotypes of Germans in the American media.

This cohesive, politically conservative element among the German-Americans has contributed to the revival of earlier efforts to overcome the traditional highly individualistic fragmentation into numerous small clubs. New integrating organizations have been founded with centers on the East Coast, in the Midwest, and in Southern California. They provide a core of readers for the German-language periodical *Amerika Woche* which has come out in various regional editions since 1973. While many of the older German-language papers are folding, New York's *Staats-Zeitung und Herold*, the *Washington Journal*, and *Aufbau* continue in their established way.

The 1950's: Era of Encounters

In the 1950's and 1960's, over three quarters of a million Germans came to the United States. In these two decades, German immigration reached its 20th century peak before it dropped abruptly to 10,632 in the 1970's, its lowest level in 150 years. The reinforcement of the German element in the American population coincided with a period when Americans interacted more closely with Germans on the continent than ever before.

The swift turnabout in American-German relations from bitter hostility to close association within a few years after 1945 caused historians to look for reasons beyond the momentum of hardening lines of conflict between East and West. Two wars against Germany in the life-time of one generation, led in the spirit of crusades, had not worn down the substance of common bonds which had linked

Americans with Germans for three centuries. The resilience of these ties quickened the restoration of good terms between individuals and governments of the two peoples which had characterized the era before the rise of Hitler.

The degree of cooperation between the United States and the Federal Republic of Germany in the 1950's was unmatched in history. It surpassed the benign climate created by the Treaty of Amity and Commerce which was signed by Jefferson, Franklin, and Adams in 1785, committing King Frederick II of Prussia and the United States of America to a "firm, inviolable, and universal peace and sincere friendship."

The positive attitudes of the 1950's were promoted on three levels. They originated during the earliest postwar reconstruction from material and moral ruin under leading American administrators for whom the assignment to a duty had grown into personal commitment to a historic task. John J. McCloy's statesmanship as high commissioner for Germany was complemented by Mrs. McCloy's extraordinary knowledge about the German situation. Secretary of State Dean Acheson, General Lucius D. Clay, and Dr. James Bryant Conant constituted the other American "founding fathers" of the Federal Republic of Germany. They prepared the way for Konrad Adenauer, the chancellor who coordinated German recovery with the Republic's integration into the Western alliance.

Parallel to interaction between governments, concerned private citizens of both countries acted to overcome wartime estrangement. In 1952 the "Atlantic Bridge" was founded in Hamburg as an organization for the promotion of mutual understanding through conferences and seminars, corresponding to the objectives of the "American Council on Germany."

The 1950's were most conspicuous as the era of an unprecedented number of personal encounters between Americans and Germans at the level of the average citizen. In American civilian offices and military barracks in West Germany, thousands of German employees shared the working-day routine. Reporters from the U. S. noted with surprise that American G.I.s, officers and their dependents, civil servants, students and travelers felt more comfortable and welcome touring in the Rhineland and the Bavarian Alps than in any other part of Europe. Americans on duty as well as temporary visitors enjoyed sampling beergarden

Gemütlichkeit in its homeland. They observed the speed of reconstruction in the devastated cities and acknowledged a work ethic congenial to American concepts.

Many young American soldiers discovered that they also shared personal values with the Germans. Romance often led to marriage. As a rule, the German war-brides, estimated at half a million, came from the same middle-class background that predominantly sustained German immigration. They adjusted comfortably to the traditional mold of the quiet, solid, proudly Americanized citizen of German descent.

After the Federal Republic became a member of NATO in 1955, the Atlantic defense partnership effected exchanges of personnel on a large scale. They reflected an unprecedented degree of peacetime military integration between two countries. The presence of over two hundred thousand American military men and women in West Germany concurred with the stationing of German soldiers in the American South and West. At any one time, up to 4,500 members of the Federal Republic's armed forces received training in Texas, Arizona, and California. Clubs and "host families", often with ties to Germany, were active to make the young Germans feel at home during their overseas tour of duty, just as German-American clubs in the Federal Republic provided hospitality for American soldiers who wished to escape the insularity of life on a military post.

German airmen who were stationed in Huntsville, Alabama, met there with countrymen more permanently established in the United States: the engineers and scientists employed by the U. S. Army Ballistic Missile Agency. The colony of rocket specialists, popularly known as "Sauerkraut Hill," was headed by Wernher von Braun after 1950. He moved into the limelight when his agency was able to respond to the challenge of the Soviet Sputnik in 1957 with the launching of the first American satellite. As part of the subsequently founded National Aeronautics and Space Administration, von Braun and his team developed the Saturn V rocket which carried the Apollo spacecraft to the moon in 1969.

Wernher von Braun was the best known of several hundred German scientific and technical experts whose services were sequestered by American military authorities at the end of the war under the codeword "Operation Paperclip." Most of these specialists acquired citizenship and worthwhile positions in the United States. They were forerunners of the so-called "brain-drain" which moved an estimated 1,800 scientists and 5,000 technicians from West Germany to the United States in the two decades after 1950.

This group substantiated anew the reputation of technical creativity of German immigrants, who had introduced novelties like the Pennsylvania Dutch Conestoga wagon and the Kentucky rifle of the gunsmiths in Lancaster county as practical contributions in the opening of the American West. The 19th century brought to mind George Westinghouse's inventions, especially the air brake, and Johann August Roebling's Brooklyn Bridge. The bridge-builder's masterpiece was opened in 1883 in time for the German-Americans' Bicentennial celebrations. In the following century, dirigibles appearing over Manhattan in 1928 demonstrated the concept of Count Zeppelin who had awed his comrades in the Civil War with his ascent in a balloon.

In the sciences as well as in the humanities, the 1950's reinvigorated academic connections between the United States and Germany of over a hundred years' duration. Official and private organizations of both countries began to offer a wide range of opportunities for the renewal of acquaintance between their academic communities. Exchanges of professors and students under the Fulbright Program were extended to the Federal Republic of Germany when the German-American Culture Agreement was signed in 1952. The German Academic Exchange Service put a significant part of its resources at the disposal of Americans heading for study and research in the Federal Republic. Long-established institutions like the Alexander von Humboldt Foundation provided support for American scholars by 1953; the Carl Duisberg Society served exchanges in applied fields of technology and economics.

On the level of secondary education, efforts to provide American and German high school students with the experience of overseas schooling were also shared by both countries. German teenagers were included in the exchange programs of the American Field Service and of other organizations promoting international understanding. GAPP—the German American Partnership Program—experimented successfully with a new approach. American teachers of German in the United States took turns with German teachers of English in the Federal Republic escorting groups of their students overseas, in a temporary exchange of schools and parental homes.

Internationally-minded clubs on both sides of the Atlantic and partnerships between nearly 50 American and German cities still aim to preserve the spirit of friendly encounters of the 1950's under more difficult conditions created by changes in international political constellations. In the 1980's, American and German young people are separated from their parents by an unusually wide personal generation gap. Besides, they failed to share the parental experience of political emergencies which held together the countries of the West in past decades, strengthening transatlantic ties. To uphold former levels of familiarity and understanding between the younger generation of both countries, the governments of the United States and West Germany decided to support an expansion of contacts. In January 1982, they each appointed a special representative to coordinate these efforts.

Different Traits in a Familiar Image

The end of the third century of German immigration marked a significant break in its continuity and in its traditional patterns. The characteristic steady flow of newcomers from Germany came virtually to a halt. The stabilization of German society and the material affluence of the early 1970's neutralized America's appeal as the "land of boundless opportunities." The citizens of the Federal Republic of Germany did not have to look across the ocean for the land of freedom when they could trust civil liberties and social security in their own democratic state.

At the time when only a negligible number of Germans intended to let down roots permanently in the United States, a large group of temporary residents from West Germany had a noticeable impact on the American economy. Thousands of businessmen followed the German mark on its way across the Atlantic when the dollar softened after 1973 and previous large-scale acquisition of West German companies and factories by American investors found its equivalent in German investments in the United States.

This concentration of German business expertise in America was an unprecedented phenomenon. Timidity in monetary enterprise was typical of the early settlers. Solid but credulous leaders like Pastorius were no match for clever lawyers in Philadelphia who had maneuvered the Frankfurt Land Company out of the fruit of their investments by 1700. The average overly cautious German immigrant of following generations was characterized by an observer: "taking fewer chances in the lottery of life than his enterprising Scotch-Irish or limber-minded Yankee neighbor, he has drawn from it fewer prizes, but also fewer blanks."

In spite of the consensus about a general lack of boldness in financial ventures, the German-American community could point to leaders in business. The life of John Jacob Astor, a butcher's son from Walldorf near Heidelberg, was the dream of a poor immigrant come true. He arrived in New York in 1763 with seven flutes as his only possession. By trading in fur, investing in real estate, and much tough wheeling and dealing, he became one of the richest men of his time. He donated $400,000 to the forerunner of New York's public library, and remembered his origins by leaving $20,000 to the German Society for Aid to Immigrants.

In the following century, German-American business dynasties were founded by Charles Spreckels from Hanover, California's "Sugar King," and Frederick Weyerhaeuser, the "Lumber King." His enterprise is still inspired by the traditional affinity of German immigrants for forests and forestry. The company of H. John Heinz, Pittsburgh's "Pickle King," is also flourishing to this day. One of his heirs and namesakes was elected United States Senator in 1976, carrying on German-American traditions in the Republican Party, in a combination of economic and political leadership.

A turn of the century precedent for international banking in America, originating from a firm in Germany, was set by Paul Moritz Warburg. Formerly a partner in the Hamburg-based family banking house, his marriage to Nina Loeb in 1895 associated him with one of the German-Jewish banking empires in New York and gave him the platform to become instrumental in the centralization of American banking through the Federal Reserve System.

German commercial banks with international corporate ties were in the vanguard of the German business migration to Manhattan in the 1970's. The consequent increase in economic integration of the United States and West Germany came at a time when the two countries' political cooperation became subject to forces of stress which had developed in the U.S.–European alliance. While

European and American economic interests were not always identical, the German and American economies became more intertwined. Over a thousand branches, affiliates, and subsidiaries of West German companies, from chemicals and pharmaceutics to textiles, improved America's balance of payments by approximately ten billion dollars. In names and ways of conducting business, these companies stress their American character. *Volkswagen of America* still draws on nostalgia for the 1950's when American servicemen took their enthusiasm for the "beetle" home with them from assignments overseas, but the company cultivates a strictly American image.

American subsidiaries of German companies have mainly settled in the southeastern states for their centers of production. In their headquarters in Manhattan, the cosmopolitan managers of these plants are as indistinguishable a part of the business scene as in Frankfurt or Tokyo. They blend in perfectly with their American surroundings in an age when the Western industrialized nations have developed almost interchangeable life-styles.

Germantown's Heirs

The emphasis in the encounters of Americans and Germans throughout three centuries shifted frequently. The wide range of German immigrants, of groups and individuals, made variety rather than uniformity characteristic of their contributions. At the same time, continuity was more striking than change in the history of German immigration. In the personality and in the fate of Francis Daniel Pastorius precedents were set for millions of his countrymen who were to follow in his footsteps, touching upon all major fields of endeavor of the Germans in America.

Pastorius considered himself a man of destiny. His salute to the descendants of Germantown, the "Future Men of Germanopolis," proved prophetic. In the translation of the *Pennsylvania Pilgrim* by the Quaker poet John Greenleaf Whittier, Pastorius sums up the epic of German migration to America in a call to posterity:

> "... Let the young generations yet to be look kindly upon this.
> Think how your fathers left their native land...
> and where the wild beast roams
> in patience planned
> New forest homes beyond the mighty sea,
> There undisturbed and free
> To live as brothers of one family..."

As unpretentious but reliable members of the American family, the men and women of Germanopolis increased in numbers, making millions of new homes, far above their pioneer fathers' expectations. The young generations received the coveted life in undisturbed freedom. They gave in exchange patient planning, plodding, and occasional impatient prodding, working in concord with their brothers to master the realities of the American dream.

Acknowledgments, Bibliography

A travel grant from the German Academic Exchange Service in New York for the spring of 1981 enabled me to use archives in Krefeld, Stuttgart, and Kaiserslautern, West Germany, in search of new material on the earliest German migration to North America.

The examination of my manuscript by scholars in the field of German-American studies was indispensable to my efforts in condensing a vast body of information into a few brief chapters. I am grateful for suggestions from Patricia Herminghouse of Washington University, St. Louis, Gerhard Weiss of the University of Minnesota, and Maria Wagner of Rutgers University. I am doubly indebted to LaVern Rippley of St. Olaf College, Minnesota, for giving my study the benefit of scrutiny by an experienced generalist in German-American history, after having added to the substance of my work with his book on *The German-Americans* (Boston, 1976). Thanks are due to my colleague at Clarion University of Pennsylvania, Ronald Shumaker, for reading copy, to the university's Board for Support of Research and President Thomas Bond for securing technical and clerical assistance. I appreciate the editorial efforts of Dr. Heinz Schneppen of the German Information Center, New York.

The selection of source material was eased by the work of Don Heinrich Tolzmann and of Stephen Benjamin, bibliographers of German Americana. This survey, like all other studies of the Germans in America, rests on the basis of Albert Faust's classic, *The German Element in the United States* (2 vol., Boston, 1909, reprinted New York, 1969). My perception of Pastorius' time is founded to a great extent on the prolific scholarship of the late 19th century, mainly Oswald Seidensticker, *Die erste deutsche Einwanderung in Amerika und die Gründung von Germantown 1683* (Philadelphia 1883); Julius Friedrich Sachse, *The German Pietists of Provincial Pennsylvania* (Philadelphia, 1895, reprinted New York, 1970); Samuel Whitaker Pennypacker, *The Settlement of Germantown, Pennsylvania, and the Beginning of German Immigration to North America* (New York, 1899, reissued 1970); Marion Dexter Learned, *The Life of Francis Daniel Pastorius, the Founder of Germantown* (Philadelphia, 1908).

Among more recent publications, Carl Wittke's *We Who Built America. The Saga of the Immigrant* (Cleveland, 1939, revised 1964), was consulted for its view of German immigration in the context of all ethnic groups' experience. Authors chosen for their treatment of specific facets of German cultural contributions include Karl J.R. Arndt and May Olson, *The German Language Press of the Americas* vol. 3 (Munich, 1980); Anneliese Harding in *America through the Eyes of German Immigrant Painters* (Boston, 1975/76); Joachim Radkau, *Die deutsche Emigration in den USA* (Düsseldorf, 1971); Gerard Wilk, *Americans from Germany* (New York, 1976). The interpretation of German-American relations after 1945 is based largely on my own research, published in *Deutschland, Soll und Haben; Amerikas Deutschlandbild* (München, 1964).

Christine M. Totten
Clarion, Pennsylvania

Index

Academy of Jewish
  Studies 46
Acheson, Dean 69
Adams, John 69
Adenauer, Konrad 69
Adler, Kurt Herbert 24
Alabama, State of 70
Albers, Josef 27, 31
Albers, Anni 27
Altgeld, John Peter 50
Altman, Benjamin 45
American Council on
  Germany 69
American Field
  Service 71
Amish 6, 47, 67
Anheuser, Eberhard 62
Anneke, Mathilde
  Giesler 15
Arendt, Hannah 39
Arion choral society 22
Astor, John Jacob 73
Atlantic Bridge 69
Austria, Austrians 23,
  30, 39, 61

Bach, Johann Sebastian
  19, 22
Baden, Germany 43
Baltimore, Maryland 13,
  20, 21, 37, 45
Bancroft, George 36
Baptists 8, 13, 16, 42
Bauhaus 27, 28
Bausch & Lomb 12
Bavaria, Germany 28,
  43, 62, 67, 69
Beck, Carl 36
Beckmann, Max 31
Beethoven, Ludwig van
  20, 23, 33
Beissel, Johann Conrad
  13, 17, 18, 26, 28
Berlin, Germany 23, 24,
  25, 27, 33, 38, 66
Bethlehem, Pennsylvania
  18, 19
Bierstadt, Albert 29, 30
Blacks 50, 56, 57,
  58, 66
Bonhoeffer, Dietrich 44
B'nai B'rith,
  Bundesbrüder 46
Boltzius, John M. 58
Boston, Massachusetts
  20, 22, 24, 45, 58
Brahms, Johannes 23
von Braun, Wernher 70
Brecht, Bertolt 24, 34
Breslau, Silesia 21, 50
Breuer, Marcel 28

Brosius, George 37
Brooklyn Bridge 71
Bruehl, Elizabeth
  Young 39
Buffalo, New York 21
Busch, Adolphus 62
Busch, Wilhelm 52

California, State of
  23, 33, 62, 63, 68,
  70, 73
Canada 67
Carl Duisberg Society 71
Catholic Church 42,
  43, 46
Charleston, South
  Carolina 21, 53
Chicago, Illinois 16,
  21, 23, 24, 25, 27,
  39, 50
Cincinnati, Ohio 16, 21,
  22, 43, 45, 60
Clay, Lucius D. 69
Cleveland, Ohio 21,
  22, 24
Cogswell, Joseph 36
Columbia University 32
Columbus, Ohio 21, 37
Conant, James B. 69
Conestoga Wagons
  63, 71
Cooper, James F. 30
Cornell University 38

Damrosch, Leopold
  21, 22
Damrosch, Walter 22
Delaware River 9
Democrats, Democratic
  Party 50, 51
Deutschamerikanischer
  Volksbund 49
Dietrich, Marlene 25,
  33, 34
Dirks, Rudolf 52
Dock, Christopher 36
Drexel, Julius 62
Dunkers, German Baptist
  Brethren 13, 17,
  26, 52
Düsseldorf, Germany
  28, 29, 60
Dutch 7, 8, 10, 41,
  42, 56

East Prussians 67
English 6, 7, 9, 10, 41,
  42, 48, 56, 61
Einhorn, David 45
Einstein, Albert 23,
  34, 39

Eisenhower, Dwight D.,
  President 56
Ephrata, Pennsylvania
  13, 17, 26, 28, 52
Epstein, Klaus 41
Expressionist painters 31

Falkner, Justus 17
Fassbinder, Rainer
  Werner 25
Federal Republic of
  Germany (also West
  Germany) 22, 23, 30,
  31, 40, 46, 64, 69,
  70, 71, 72, 73, 74
Feininger, Lyonel 28, 31
Feuchtwanger, Lion 34
Follen, Carl 36, 58
Francke, August
  Hermann 36
Frankenberg, Caroline
  Louise 37
Frankfurt on the Main 7,
  8, 9, 32, 40, 42, 47,
  48, 54, 59, 74
Frankfurt Land Company
  8, 73
Franklin, Benjamin 14,
  17, 27, 38, 69
Franklin and Marshall
  College 43
Freethinkers 42, 44
Frick, Henry Clay 12
Froebel, Friedrich 37, 49
Froebel, Julius 49

GAPP—German
  American Partnership
  Program 71
Gehrig, Lou 37
George, Manfred 16
Georgia, State of 18,
  52, 58
German Academic
  Exchange Service 71
German-Jewish 16, 21,
  38, 45, 46, 63, 73
Germania Orchestra 20
German-language press
  13, 14, 15, 16, 58,
  64, 68
German Marshall Fund
  of the U.S. 64
Germantown,
  Pennsylvania 6-10,
  12, 13, 16, 17, 26,
  29, 31, 35, 36, 41,
  48, 56, 57, 58, 59,
  60, 62, 63, 66, 75

Gildersleeve, Basil L. 38
(von) Goethe, Johann
    Wolfgang 34, 60
Göttingen, Germany
    36, 38
Grass, Günter 25
Graupner, Gottlieb 20
Gropius, Walter 27
Gray, Hanna Holborn 41

Hamburg, Germany 40,
    69, 73
Halle, Germany 36,
    42, 43
Hanover (Hannover),
    Germany 20, 73
Harvard University 27,
    32, 36, 40, 58, 62
Hayes, Maria Ludwig 54
Hayes, Rutherford B.,
    President 49
Hebrew Union College
    45
Hecker, Friedrich 21, 55
Heidelberg, Germany
    38, 46, 73
Heinz, H. John 73
Heinzen, Karl 15, 58
Hemingway, Ernest 25
Henni, Johann Martin 43
Herckheimer, Nicolaus
    (Herkimer, Nicholas) 53
Herrnhuter
    Brüdergemeinde
    (see also Moravians)
    18, 19, 59
Herzog, Werner 25
Hesse (Hessen),
    Germany 50
Hessians 55
Hindemith, Paul 23
Hitler, Adolf 23, 33, 34,
    39, 46, 49, 69
Holborn, Hajo 41
Holborn, Louise W. 41
Hollerith, Herman 14
Hollywood, California
    25, 33
Hoover, Herbert,
    President 64
Huber, Johann 12
von Humboldt,
    Wilhelm 38
Alexander von Humboldt
    Foundation 71
Hutterites 47

Illinois, State of 33, 55
Illinois Institute of
    Technology 27
Indians 18, 30, 41, 42
—Lenni Lenape 59
—Iriquois 60
—Mohawk 60

Iowa, State of 24
Irish 6, 41, 43, 44, 46,
    48, 52, 66
Israel 46
Italians 41, 66, 68

Jacobi, Abraham 45
Jefferson, Thomas,
    President 69
Jewish Reformed 45, 46
Jews 42, 45, 46
Johns Hopkins
    University 38
Johnson, Alwin 39
Johnson, Andrew,
    President 58

Kahn, Otto H. 45
de Kalb, Johann 53
Kansas, State of 21, 67
Kassel, Germany 31
Kelpius (Magister), Johann
    17, 18
Kennedy, John Fitzgerald,
    President 27, 60
Kentucky, State of 71
Keurlis, Peter 62
Kissinger, Henry 41
Klemm, Johann
    Gottfried 19
Klemperer, Otto 23
Kohler, Kaufmann 45
Koerner, Gustav 15, 55
Know-Nothing, Nativist
    movement 44, 48, 58
Krefeld (Crefeld),
    Germany 6, 8, 9, 10,
    35, 48, 52, 56
Kriegsheim (Crisheim),
    Germany 8, 9, 10
Krimmel, Johann
    Ludwig 29
Kuhn, Fritz Julius 49

Laemmle, Carl 25
Lafayette, Marquis de 53
Lang, Fritz 25
Lehmann, Lotte 24
Leinsdorf, Erich 24
Leisler, Jacob 9
Leo Baeck Institute 46
Leutze, Emmanuel
    29, 30
Lieber, Franz (Francis) 32,
    33, 34, 36
Liederkranz choral
    society 22
Lincoln, Abraham,
    President 32, 49,
    51, 55
Liszt, Franz 21
Loeb, Nina 73
Loeb, Solomon 45

Los Angeles, California
    23, 24
Louisville, Kentucky 21
Lubitsch, Ernst 25
Ludwig, Christopher 54
Luther, Martin 16, 17,
    43, 61
Lutheran Church 12, 17,
    42, 44

Mahler, Gustav 23
Mainz, Germany
    12, 62
Mann, Heinrich 33, 34
Mann, Thomas 17, 34
McCloy, John J. 69
Manheim, Pennsylvania
    12
Marcuse, Ludwig 34
Marshall Plan 64
Maryland, State of 28,
    53, 61
Massachusetts, State of
    6, 36, 58
May, Karl 30
Mendelssohn-Bartholdy,
    Felix 22
Mennonites 8, 12, 36,
    42, 47, 48, 52,
    56, 67
Mergenthaler, Ottmar 13
Methodists 18, 42
Mies van der Rohe,
    Ludwig 27
Miller, Heinrich (Henry) 13
Milwaukee, Wisconsin
    16, 21, 22, 36, 37,
    43, 60, 62
Minneapolis, Minnesota
    20, 21
Minuit (Minnewit),
    Peter 9
Missouri, State of 33,
    49, 55, 62
Missouri Synod 44
Moravians (see also
    Herrnhuter Brüderge-
    meinde) 18, 19, 46,
    52, 59
Mozart, Wolfgang
    Amadeus 23
Mühlenberg, Heinrich
    Melchior (Muhlen-
    berg, Henry) 42, 52
Muhlenberg, John Peter
    Gabriel 52
Mühlheim, Germany
    10, 12
Müller (Miller), Peter
    17, 18
Munich (München),
    Germany 22, 28,
    29, 30, 31

Nast, Thomas 51, 52
New Braunfels, Texas 33
New School for Social
　Research, NY 39
New York—City 19, 20,
　21, 23, 24, 27, 29,
　32, 35, 37, 45, 46,
　51, 63, 64, 73
—State of 12, 50, 53,
　54, 64
—Staats-Zeitung &
　Herold 15, 16, 64, 68
—Symphony 21, 22
Niebuhr, Reinhold 44
Nimitz, Chester W. 56
North Carolina, State
　of 52

Oberlander, Gustav 64
Ochs, Adolph S. 45
Olmsted, Frederick Law
　33
Oppenheimer, Julius
　Robert 39
Ottendörfer (Ottendorfer)
　Anna and Oswald 64
Otto, Frederick
　(Friedrich) 19

Pabst brewers 22, 62
Palatinate (Pfalz),
　Germany 8, 10, 14,
　43, 47, 51, 56, 60,
　61, 64
Panofsky, Erwin 40
Pastorius, Franz Daniel
　(Francis Daniel) 6-9,
　12, 26, 31, 32, 33,
　34, 35, 36, 41, 42,
　48, 52, 56, 59, 63,
　66, 73, 75
Penn, William 7-9, 32,
　48, 59
Pennsylvania, State of 8,
　10, 12-14, 16-18, 28,
　41, 42, 47, 52, 53,
　57, 60, 75
Pennsylvania Dutch
　(designation for Penn-
　sylvania Germans) 10,
　26, 28, 37, 63,66-
　67, 71
Pestalozzi, Johann
　Heinrich 36
Philadelphia, Pennsyl-
　vania 6, 7, 9, 10, 12,
　14, 20, 22, 28, 29,
　32, 35, 36, 42, 48,
　56, 66, 73
Pietists 7, 8, 42
Pittsburgh, Pennsylvania
　12, 21, 37, 73
Poles 41, 68

Postl, Karl (Charles
　Sealsfield) 30
Preminger, Otto 25
Princeton University
　34, 40
Princeton Institute for
　Advanced Study 39
Protestants 41, 42, 43,
　46, 58
Prussia, Germany 21,
　25, 53
Puritans 17, 60, 61

Quakers 7, 8, 10, 14,
　17, 35, 42, 52, 56,
　75

Rapp, George 16, 47
Reformed Church
　(German Reformed
　Church) 42, 43
Reform Judaism 45
Reinhardt, Max 25
Reisinger, Hugo 62
Remarque, Erich
　Maria 25
Republicans, Republican
　Party 48, 49, 50, 51,
　55, 73
Reuther, Walter 51
Rhineland 6-10, 12, 14,
　27, 29, 30, 43, 64,
　66, 67, 69
Rittenhouse, William
　(Ruttinghausen,
　Wilhelm) 12
Rockefeller, John D. 38
Rockefeller, Peter 38
Roebling, Johann August
　71
Roosevelt, Franklin D.,
　President 51
Roosevelt, Theodore,
　President 22, 52, 55
Rosenwald, Julius 45
Rosicrucians 13, 17
Russian-Germans 67
Ruth, Babe 37

Santa Barbara,
　California 24
San Francisco, California
　21, 24, 63
Saur (Sauer, Sower),
　Christopher 12-14, 36
Saur, Maria 13
Saxony, Germany 17, 19
Scandinavians 41, 61
Schaeffer, Herman 37
Schiff, Jacob H. 45
Schiller, Friedrich 24
Schlitz brewers 62

Schlöndorff, Volker 25
Schönberg, Arnold 24
Schumann, Clara 21
Schurman, Jacob Gould
　38
Schurz, Carl 15, 37, 45,
　49, 51, 52, 55, 58,
　60, 64, 66
Schurz, Margarethe M.
　37
Schwab, Charles 12
Schwenkfelder 18
Scots 41
Scotch-Irish 10, 48, 73
Seelig, J. Gottfried 13
Sigel, Franz 55
Silesians 67
Sommerhausen, Germany
　10
Spaatz, Carl 55
Spreckels, Carl 73
Stern, Fritz 41
von Sternberg, Josef 25
Stiegel, Heinrich W. 12
St. Louis, Missouri
　16, 20, 21, 43, 55,
　60, 62
Steinitz, Hans 16
Steinmetz, Charles
　Proteus 50
Steinway, Henry
　(Steinweg, Heinrich
　Engelhard) 19
von Steuben, Friedrich
　Wilhelm 53, 64, 66
Strauss, Levi 63
Strauss, Richard 22
Sudeten Germans 67
Sullivan, Louis Henry 27
Swabia (see also
　Württemberg,
　Germany) 25, 67
Swedes 9, 17, 42, 59
Switzerland and Swiss
　23, 28, 36, 43, 47,
　56, 67
Syberberg, Hans-Jürgen
　25

Texas, State of 21, 24,
　33, 70
Theosophical Brethren
　(Society of the Woman
　in the Wilderness,
　Rosicrucians) 17
Thomas, Theodore 20,
　21
Tillich, Paul 44
Transcendentalists 44
Turner Societies 36, 37,
　44, 51, 55
Tyroleans 61, 67

Unitarians 44
United States of America 6, 15, 16, 20, 25, 30, 32, 34, 37-38, 39, 43, 61, 63, 64, 67, 69, 71-74

Vermont, State of 33
Vienna (Wien), Austria 23, 24, 25
Villard, Henry (Hilgard, Heinrich) 15
Virginia, State of 8, 28, 53, 60
Volkswagen of America 74

Wagner, John Peter 37
Wagner, Richard 21, 22, 23
Wagner, Robert 50
Wagner, Wolfgang 23
Waldseemüller, Martin 8

Walter, Bruno (Schlesinger) 23
Warburg, Paul Moritz 73
Washington, D.C. 29
Washington, George, President 19, 29, 42, 52, 53, 54
Watertown, Wisconsin 37
Weill, Kurt 24
Weimar, Germany 27
—Republic 23
Weiser, Johann Conrad 60
Wendt, Mathilde 15
Werfel, Franz 34
Wesley, John 18
Westphalia, Germany 43, 45
Westinghouse, George 71
Weyerhaeuser, Frederik 73
White, Andrew 38

Whittier, John Greenleaf 75
Wilder, Billy 25
Winston-Salem, North Carolina 19
Wise, Isaac Mayer 45
Wright, Frank Lloyd 27
Württemberg, Germany (see also Swabia) 13, 26, 29, 43

Yale University 23
Yiddish 47

Zenger, Peter 14, 15
Zeppelin, Count Ferdinand 71
Zinzendorf, Count, N.L. 18, 52, 59
Zuckmayer, Carl 33
Zweig, Stefan 34